The essence of Dōgen

The essence of Dōgen

Masanobu Takahashi
Translated by Yuzuru Nobuoka

Kegan Paul International
London, Boston and Melbourne

First published in 1983
by Kegan Paul International Ltd
39 Store Street,
London WC1E 7DD,
9 Park Street,
Boston, Mass. 02108, USA, and
296 Beaconsfield Parade, Middle Park,
Melbourne, 3206, Australia
Set in Press Roman by
Hope Services, Abingdon, Oxon.
and printed in Great Britain by
Hartnoll Print
Bodmin, Cornwall

Library of Congress Cataloging in Publication Data

Takahashi, Masanobu, 1909-
The essence of Dōgen.
Includes index.
1. Dōgen, 1200-1253.   I. Dōgen, 1200-1253.
Selections. 1983.   II. Title.
BQ9449.D657T35 1983   294.3'927'0924   82-21324

ISBN 0-7103-0046-8 (U.S.)

Contents

Contents

Preface

This book is meant for the English reader who wishes to study the thought of Dōgen, one of the greatest *Zen* Masters of Japan's Middle Ages. Because of this objective, I mention in greater detail matters which may seem familiar or unnecessary for the Japanese reader. Especially for the academically oriented individual, I attempt to formulate a theoretical systematization of Dōgen's thought set into the cultural fabric of Japan.

This orientation towards a methodical ordering of Dōgen's thinking has been a constant concern from the earliest days of my study of this great *Zen* Master. *The Structure of the Practical Ethics of Dōgen's Philosophy* which I published at Sankibō-Busshorin Tokyo, in 1967, was the result of a ten year study on this subject. In this work, I offered an essential systematization of Dōgen's thought. In 1978, I published another book, *The Precepts of Dōgen — Their synthetic Interpretation*, Risō-sha, Tokyo. This was the result of a more elaborate and deeper study covering the same ground. With this latter book, I believe that almost the entire structure of Dōgen's thought has been brought to light in a precise, theoretical analysis.

Now in this book, intended for the English speaking reader, I set out to explain Dōgen's thought in the light of my two previous studies as systematically as possible in concise, unequivocal language, while avoiding intricate, rambling explanations. I must add that I have not forgotten to add new insights drawn from my on-going studies. It has been a new discovery for me how the mysteries of Buddhism are at work at the deepest level of the *Shōbōgenzō*, Dōgen's greatest and most important work of all. You will find this discussed in the theory of *kū* (emptiness) and the material on a practical philosophy based on *kū* found in Chapter 4.

I should also say that when considering the audience for this book, I made it a principle that the Chinese characters quoted here, for example, the names of books or persons as well as Chinese set phrases should be pronounced in the Japanese way. I think it better that any person who wishes to study Japanese culture become accustomed to the Japanese way of reading Chinese characters as soon as possible. The true significance of the Japanese classics, a product of a delicate and refined speculation will never be grasped thoroughly unless they are reviewed in their original language. It is expected that the student of Dōgen should master Japanese and peruse the basic texts in the original language. The Supplement of this book is provided for such adventurous students.

I wish to express my profound thanks to Professor Yuzuru Nobuoka at Onomichi Junior College, Hiroshima for his careful and laborious work of translating my Japanese manuscript. I highly appreciate his linguistic ability as well as his wide knowledge of literature and religious philosophy, both oriental and occidental, which brought forth this faithful and lucid translation. I am heartily satisfied with the result.

My thanks also go to Professor Maureen O'Brien of Notre Dame Seishin University, Okayama and Instructor Piers H. T. Dowding of Okayama College of Commerce, who in the process of translation cooperated with the translator by refining the English and offering many valuable suggestions.

Lastly I wish to acknowledge a particular debt to my friend, Dr Imahori Seiji, president of Hiroshima Women's College. Without his encouraging response to this book as it was being written and his kind offer to arrange things with the publisher for me, the publication of this book would have been impossible.

Dr Masanobu Takahashi
August 1981

Acknowledgments

I wish to acknowledge my debt of gratitude to the translators of the following works by Dōgen; their skill made my task all that simpler. *Shōbōgenzō*, vol. I, translated by Nishiyama Kosen and John Stevens, Daihokkaikaku, Tokyo, 1975. *Shōbōgenzō*, vol. II, translated by Nishiyama Kosen and John Stevens, Nakayama-shobō, Tokyo, 1977. *The First Step to Dōgen's Zen* — *Shōbōgenzō-Zuimonki*, translated by Yokoi Yūhō, Sankibō-busshorin, Tokyo, 1972. *Shōbōgenzō-Zuimonki*, translated by Kodani Teruo, a private press edition, Tottori, 1968. *Dōgen's Formative Years in China — An Historical Study and Annotated Translation of the Hōkyō-ki*, Takashi James Kodera, Routledge & Kegan Paul, London and Henley, 1980. The *Busshō (Buddha-nature)*, section of the *Shōbōgenzō* translated by Yokoi Yūhō, a *Bulletin* of the Research Institute of *Zen* of Aichi-gakuin University, Nagoya, no. 8, 1977.

I also have to express my heartful thanks to Sr Maureen O'Brien, Professor at Notre Dame Seishin University, Okayama, and Instructor Piers H. T. Dowding of Okayama College of Commerce who have not only looked over and corrected my translations but also given many useful suggestions. Without their help I could not have completed this difficult task.

In the translation of the titles of Dōgen's works, Buddhist and Zen terms, Chinese set phrases, and the like, I tried to express their true meaning as accurately as possible, evading the mere superficial word-by-word rendition. I spent many hours with the author discussing the problems in order to find the most suitable English expression. According to the author's intention, I give Japanese personalities in Japanese fashion, that is, with the family name preceding the personal name.

The author has long cherished the wish of introducing Dōgen to the West. I would be very pleased if my translation can fulfil the author's wish and make some contribution to the correct understanding by the West of this great *Zen* philosopher of Japan.

Yuzuru Nobuoka

August 1981

Chapter 1

Dōgen's life and his essential precepts

1 Dōgen's life

Dōgen was born on 26 January in AD 1200 and died on 29 September in 1253. An outline of his 54 years of life is as follows.[1] He was born into an aristocratic family and was related to the Emperor. His father was the Lord Keeper of the Privy Seal and his mother, the daughter of a certain Regent. But Dōgen lost both parents early; the former when he was 3 years old; the latter when he was 8. After the loss of his parents he was brought up by a maternal uncle. His lot was not good as such but he was given an excellent education worthy of nobility. As he showed brilliant talent at an early age, he was considered to be a boy wonder. Observing his ability, his foster father intended preparing him for a successful career in officialdom, but Dōgen wished to enter the Buddhist priesthood. At 14 years of age, he freely renounced the world. For about four years he devoted himself to the study of traditional Buddhism; at the age of 18, dissatisfied with this, he entered a monastery of the *Rinzai Zen* sect, which had just been introduced from China. There he remained for about six years and at the age of 24, went to the China of the Sung Dynasty (960-1279) to deepen his study. In China he made a profound, many faceted probing into *Zen*. The practical result was that he was both impressed and affected by the *Sōtō-Zen* sect. He finally established his religious thought, based upon the tenets and practices of *Sōtō-Zen*. Returning to Japan at the age of 28, he began to preach and subsequently became the founder of the *Sōtō* sect in Japan.

At first Dōgen resided at a *Zen* temple in Kyoto called *Kennin-ji*. After three years he moved to the suburbs, founding the temple of *Kōshō-ji* (he was now 34 years old). For ten years he engaged in teaching and working for the spread of his faith, but at 44 years of age, driven

1

by the stress of circumstances, he moved to Echizen, a remote area about 200 kilometres north of Kyoto. He founded a temple there, named it *Eihei-ji*, and continued missionary work until he was 54 years old. In the autumn of his fifty-fourth year, becoming ill, he went to Kyoto for medical treatment, but soon, all remedies having proved ineffectual, this great *Zen* thinker died.

2 Shikan-taza (single-minded zazen)

Dōgen lived in the early half of the Kamakura era (1192–1333) of Japanese history. It was a time when radical societal changes were underway, due to the change from an aristocratic to a military government. Shaking itself free of the troublesome formalism which imitated the political and social pattern of the Tang Dynasty of China, Japan began to display characteristics proper to itself, while setting a new value on certain fundamental elements in life. This tendency gave rise to many new sects of Buddhism. Traditional Buddhism, as a religion for noblemen, had degenerated into a kind of esoteric practice or collection of magical rites. In contrast to this, the Buddhism of this new age celebrated a return to the truth of Buddhism. Transforming itself into a fundamentalist religion for the common people, it directed itself towards becoming easily attainable and simply understood.

Broadly speaking, there were three main sects central to this new Buddhism: the *Nembutsu* sect, the *Zen* sect, and the *Nichiren* sect. The first, the *Nembutsu* sect teaches that we can be born into the Land of Happiness by faithfully chanting a *nembutsu* (prayer) to Buddha. Three minor sects are offshoots of this branch of Buddhism: *Jōdo-shū, Shinshū*, and *Ji-shū*. The second, the *Zen* sect, lays special stress on *zazen*, a paradoxical act of sitting without thinking and yet, not without thinking; a paradox which involves moving beyond thought. Although *zazen* is assiduously practised, the essential spirit of *Zen* is its belief in *Jihi*, the mercy of Buddha. The doctrine of *Jihi*, it should be noted, is the point at which all three sects converge. The third, the *Nichiren* sect, emphasizes that man can be saved simply by reciting the titles of the important Sutras in which they have faith.

Dōgen's *Sōtō* sect is one of the sects which belongs to the *Zen* sect and its characteristic is that it accentuates *zazen* more than anything else. *Shikan-taza* (a single-minded sitting in *zazen*) which Dōgen advocates is the best expression of this teaching. It means 'to sit intently with a single-mindedness'. That is to say, we can find the true way to enlightenment if we just sit. We find in this teaching an attitude quite contrary to the trivialities and difficulties of the old, conventional Buddhism. Buddhism formerly demanded troublesome practices and the ability of the believer to understand complex esoteric theories, far beyond the grasp of uneducated believers. '*Zazen* only', however, caused a revolutionary change in this situation; the *Way* became attainable to all, the *Way* was simplified and became 'familiar'. The original preaching of Buddha was identical to Kamakura Buddhism in its accessibility to all, and for this reason it was reactionary.

Among the plethora of teachings, Dōgen's shows the strongest tendency to return to the true, original spirit of Buddha. The precepts of Buddha contain some theory; they are not always illogical though certainly an appeal is made to a certain supraintellectual sense rather than the rigid strictures of logic. A person may arrive at or grasp the truth not as a result of logical reasoning but through an enlightenment which does not negate the role of intellect. This is what *satori* in Buddhism means, and the faculty for attaining this is called wisdom. Dōgen does not always ignore the need for disciplining such wisdom, but his opinion is that if the mind returns to its pure, original beginning, it will be able to exercise this wisdom properly. Assisting the mind to return to its original state is of the essence of *zazen*.

To explore this central point in Dōgen's teaching, two of his works are helpful. One is *Fukan-zazengi* (*General Promotion of the Ways of Zazen*) and the other is *Shōbōgenzō* (*The Treasury which Contains the True and Essential Teaching of Buddhism*). The former, only one volume in length, was completed during the year he returned from China. We may call it a kind of manifesto which declares the establishment of the *Sōtō* sect, based on the practice of *zazen*. In order to spread his teachings and explain them more easily, he wrote another volume, entitled *Bendōwa* (*An Introduction to the Way of Zazen*). Both books explain the physical reality of *zazen* as a practice where one sits cross-legged, the spinal column straight, a practice by which the mind is set free, and returned to the state of activity of a pure, 'liberated' spirit. The stability of a pure placid mind acquired through *zazen* is of the essence of the 'Buddha World'. Therefore, if the student wants to keep having within himself the true nature of Buddha, the practice of *zazen* must be continued without interruption. That is to say, practice becomes one with *satori*; this is called *shushō-ittō* (*the practice is itself enlightenment*) or *honshō-myōshū* (true enlightenment is itself excellent practice). What Dōgen preaches by advocating *shikan-taza* is that everyday life should be lived in the spirit of *zazen*. This aspect of his teaching underscores the certainty of adherence to the practice of *zazen* only.

3

Is it possible, it may be argued, to be satisfied with doing only *zazen*? Are there no other important doctrines or tenets to be known? Actually, there are. Human existence raises some questions, the nature of religious belief raises others. How is Dōgen's preaching connected with Buddha's essential precepts, or how is his teaching concerned with life after death, that death which we poor mortals cannot escape? Concerning the practical phases of life, what does Dōgen think about the problem of good and evil? Does Dōgen refer to such problems and give an answer to them? Of course he does. He talks and preaches about them in various ways. Many of his literary works are the records of such explanations and preaching. Above all, the *Shōbōgenzō* is his greatest, the most important work of all. To grasp the whole structure of Dōgen's thought, we must study it with special reference to the *Shōbōgenzō* as well as to his other minor works.

There is one important point, however, which should not be forgotten or disregarded when considering the *shikan-taza* which Dōgen advocates. The ultimate meaning of *shikan-taza* is to practise *zazen* alone. Compared to the whole structure of Dōgen's thought about which he discourses at length, *shikan-taza* occupies the smallest part; 'one should do *zazen* only' means in other words, 'one should do this at least.' What is required here appears to be very little, but *shikan-taza* ranks at the top of any scale in order of importance. The summation of what Dōgen preaches is, in a sense, that we should practise nothing but *zazen*. We could even say that this teaching encapsulates the whole body of his precepts.

Essentially what *shikan-taza* aims at is a way of making Buddhism attainable, simple, and familiar in contradistinction to the erroneous approach which conventional Buddhism had tended to take and preach. What Dōgen asks is that a follower recognizes that some kind of purity and inclusiveness is found in *shikan-taza.* [2] First, such purity asks that one should not practise *zazen* from any profit-motivated type of ambition, such as that of becoming a Buddha. The truth of *shikan-taza* is 'zazen for *zazen*'s sake'. But, even if this is so, the final and ideal aim of *zazen* is to become Buddha. 'Zazen for *zazen*'s sake' can be taken to mean that enlightenment − the true nature of Buddha − is always concerned with practice; the essential quality of Buddha actualizes itself in the practice of *zazen*. Therefore we are urged to devote ourselves to *zazen* practice, during which all worldly thoughts are dispelled from the mind. *Shikan-taza* implies and demands such purity of intention. Second, inclusiveness means that all the commandments of Buddha are included in *zazen* itself. Thus *zazen* is practised for its own sake, because all the rules and commandments of Buddha can be observed by adhering to it alone.

Is it possible, however, for society to hold itself together, if we practise nothing but *zazen* in daily life, while basing such a choice on the belief that 'all the commandments of Buddha can be observed by doing *zazen* alone'? Is doing *zazen* only, in conflict with societal involvement? Dōgen is ready to answer these questions. He teaches renouncing the world, by joining the priesthood, so that one can devote oneself to *zazen*. But if everybody wanted to do that, could society survive? His teaching provides an answer to this problem. He suggests two interrelated concepts, *gūgō* and *Bosatsu-dō* (the Ways of *Bodhisattva*). *Gūgō* designates the *karma* common to all men, a concept derived from the theory of transmigration and regeneration. *Gūgō* postulates the truth that society can hold itself together through the co-operative labour of all people, such as labour being allocated according to the *karma* of each man. This idea has become one of the basic principles of Buddhism.

Originally *gūgō* was applied only to the natural world, but it may also be applied to human society according to Dōgen's free interpretation. On the other hand, *Bosatsu-dō* is 'the way' of constructing an ideal world for all humankind, a world of the Buddha encompassing even eternity. With these two concepts as a background, Dōgen encourages us to become priests, so that we can devote ourselves to *zazen* practice. One character of Dōgen's precepts is found in this explanation; society is never denied nor are the laity ever haughtily brushed aside. Whether priests or laymen, *zazen* is a universal mode of meditation.

This precept of Dōgen's is even more significant because he teaches from the standpoint of a formally religious man. For him, religion must prepare the way for the salvation of all human beings. If only the elect can be saved, religion is suspect. In this point the significance of Kamakura Buddhism's development towards becoming attainable, simple, and familiar, becomes clear. Dōgen's contribution was to teach that the practice of *zazen* opened the way to universal salvation. Indeed, if the average person had to memorize the many detailed rules or understand the profound theory of Buddhism in order to attain salvation, only a minority could entertain any hope of success. Or, if Dōgen required an understanding of the complex theory of Buddhism so that the same average individual could read the *Shōbōgenzō*, the attainment of the Way would be beyond him.

His recommendation to 'just sit in *zazen*', a method which disregarded difficult and troublesome requirements reflects the true attitude of a religious man. All men may be saved through *zazen* practice alone. All that is required of those who seek intently to achieve the attainment of salvation is to enter the priesthood or practise *zazen*. The practising of *zazen* as a *Bosatsu-dō* is a timeless practice by which the believer might not attain salvation immediately, but ultimately salvation will be attained. The compassionate quality of this Buddhist tenet also allows for the concrete historical reality that owing to various situations and circumstances a person may be prevented from beginning *zazen*. But he or she will have a chance to do so sometime according to the theory of the transmigration of souls. In conclusion, it is possible to see that *shikan-taza* is an irreducible, minimum demand put forth by Dōgen — as evidenced by the terse comment that 'one should do at least this.' Any reading of the *Shōbōgenzō* should bear this in mind.

The core of Dōgen's preaching is the practice of *zazen*. The practice of *zazen* knows no human limit and can be practised according to an individual's will and ability. Dōgen, by calling such *zazen, bendō-kufū*,[3] the practice of the Way of *zazen* to seek the Buddha's true teaching, placed it at the centre of a populist interpretation of salvation. The introductory book of *bendō-kufū* is nothing less than the *Shōbōgenzō* itself.

Chapter 2

Genjō-kōan (the actuality of instruction)

1 Kōan (instruction) and Genjō (actuality)

The most symbolic word in Dōgen's preaching is *shikan-taza*, and because of this it would be well to investigate the richness and profundity of its meaning. We can do that best by reading his various works, but especially the *Shōbōgenzō*, which is at the heart of his teachings. Scholars are unable to tell exactly how many chapters there are in the *Shōbōgenzō*; perhaps 90 in all. Dōgen began to write it at the age of 34, six years after his return from China, and he continued to write it to the end of his life. Dōgen entitled the work, *Shōbōgenzō*, at some time while writing and arranging it into 75 chapters; the other 12 chapters were added later. Tradition holds that he planned a total of 100 chapters after rearrangement and additions. We find today a collection of temporarily arranged chapters, extra chapters or anthologies compiled by his successors. Many documentation problems remain to be solved. But it is commonly agreed that Dōgen arranged the work into 75 chapters and added 12 sequences during his lifetime.

The *Shōbōgenzō* is considered by many to be a very difficult work − difficult both to read and understand. Accepting this as a given, the first question is that of what Dōgen wanted to teach through this book and what the nature of its content is. The answer is suggested to some degree by its title. *Shōbōgenzō* can be translated as 'the right teaching to be learned concerning the true and essential spirit of Buddhism'. The content is clear in an initial reading. The key term denoting the concrete reality of 'the right teaching' is above all the *genjō-kōan* (the actuality 'genjō' is instruction 'kōan').[1] How strongly Dōgen stresses the *genjō-kōan* is shown by the fact that he put the chapter on the *genjō-kōan* (c. 1233) in the first part of the *Shōbōgenzō*. Indeed, when we read the whole of

7

the *Shōbōgenzō* in detail, we can unequivocally see that the *genjō-kōan* is fundamental to every segment of this work. Moreover, the first chapter is more important for the particular reason that it was written for Yōkō-shū, one of Dōgen's laymen followers (as can be determined from the postscript of Dōgen himself).

Dōgen's primary intention was to write it solely for the layman, but, after nineteen years, when he decided to compile all his writings into one book, the *Shōbōgenzō*, he put it in as the opening chapter. The fact that Dōgen attached such importance to what he preached for the lay disciple shows that this initial section contained valuable implications which should not be overlooked, universal elements necessary not only for monks but also for anyone who wants to understand Buddhism. In fact, this chapter may well be regarded as containing core teaching which the other sections of the monumental work discuss more fully. In this sense, the study of the *genjō-kōan* can be an introduction to the essence of the *Shōbōgenzō*.

With Dōgen, the *genjō-kōan* possesses the double meaning of 'actuality is instruction' and 'to actualize instruction'. But even in the case of 'actuality is instruction', the aim is more for instruction to develop into actualization, so 'to actualize instruction' is of central import. In Dōgen's formulation what then is the meaning of *genjō* and *kōan*? Their meanings are not difficult. *Genjō* means 'a practical actualization' which comes from its literal meaning, 'to be actual'. *Kōan* is the technical term proper to *Zen* Buddhists, which means the fundamental theme of *kufū* (to seek the Buddha's true teaching). Generally the words and actions of various patriarchs of Buddhism are taken up as the theme of *kufū*. Trying to discover one's own Way while reflecting on them is true *kufū*. *Kōan* is then not only the theme of *kufū*, but also an instruction or a good example according to which we try to do *kufū*. So if we separate the *genjō-kōan* into two concepts, *genjō* and *kōan*, the latter becomes more important. When we say 'actuality is instruction' it is we, ourselves, who pursue 'actuality as instruction', and even when we say 'to actualize instruction' it is also we, ourselves, who actualize instruction. Finally by way of summation, *genjō* performs only an intermediate function between the *kōan* and the *Zen* practitioner.

2 Kōan-Zen and mokushō-Zen

From mere verbal analysis it is not proclaimed that the *kōan* has a more important meaning than *genjō*. Verbal analysis is only a clue to an understanding of the *kōan*.

As was mentioned, the *kōan* encapsulates the fundamental theme of *kufū*, an instruction or a practical example, according to which we practise the Buddha Way. Do not other sects of Buddhism have this kind of thing? Yes, they also make use of such themes. In essence the Buddhist Scriptures are a collection of instructions and examples. Every sect of Buddhism is founded on the Buddhist Scriptures or the theoretical texts attached to them. Buddhist Scriptures on which the teachings of various sects are based, we call *kyōten*. Indeed, however excellent a system of teaching not based on the Buddhist Scriptures one might establish, it could not be called Buddhism in any sense without a scriptural base. So far as it is called Buddhism, any teaching must have its source in the Scriptures. But if we are too scrupulous about commentaries written about the words of the Scriptures, they will be reduced to a mere shell stripped of all their content. *Zen* Buddhism is revolutionary in this sense, because it opened the way for us to reach the truth of the teachings of Buddha, instead of stopping at an artificial juggling of interpretations of the Scriptures. It opposed the formalism of *kyōshū*. (*Zen* Buddhists used this name to describe a Buddhism whose teachings are based on mere annotation of the words of the Scriptures.)

There arises, however, the question of how we are able to call *Zen* Buddhism 'Buddhism', if it will not adhere to the Scriptures as all other sects do, even though these sects are liable to degenerate into formalism of faith. The answer to this question can be found in one word, *ishin-denshin* (communication of mind with mind); the Master transfers the true spirit of Buddhism to his disciples without depending on the medium of language. This way of teaching was not an invention of *Zen* Buddhism. The Shakyamuni Buddha himself had used such a way in addition to the Scriptures. *Zen* Buddhism followed it. It is referred to as *kyōge-betsuden* (a transmission outside the Scriptures) or *furyū-monji* (a teaching independent of words). One of the reasons why *shikan-taza* is so important can be explained at this point, that is to say, it is a way of transmission which does not rest on any words of the Scriptures.

The rise of the *Zen* sect of Buddhism, which advocated *ishin-denshin*, seems natural, seen in the historical and theoretical context stated above. No one grasps truth or profound meaning with words, but only with the heart. The final aim of *ishin-denshin* is, of course, to arrive at the true Way of the Buddha. Any sect requires some standard according to which one can learn the Way under the Master. Such a standard, an instruction, or an example is a *kōan*. While *kyōshū* has its authority in *kyōten*, the *Zen* sect has its in the *kōan*. If the *Zen* sect had no *kōan*, it would not be accepted as Buddhism. In this sense, we must assert that the *kōan* is of utmost importance to the *Zen* sect.

The practical words and actions of the Patriarchs are taken up as a *kōan*. The student, it is believed, ought to find the true Way by reflecting on them, for both words and practice are expressions of the *Truth*. The *Zen* sect contends that we cannot grasp such *Truth*, if we are absorbed only in interpreting the words of the Scriptures. The significant parts of the various discourses of the Patriarchs have been collected then by the *Zen* Masters as *kōan*. Naturally their numbers increased from age to age. The famous *Hekigan-shū* was an anthology of such *kōan*, a collection of 100 *kōan*, with hints of *kufū*. Several other selections of *kōan* were compiled; some chose hundreds of *kōan*. The disciples tried to do *kufū*, to solve each *kōan* under the guidance of the Masters. While some could not get through even one *kōan*, others could easily pass through several in a short time. While some Masters would not easily permit their disciples to get through *kōan*, others were very permissive. In short, whether a disciple grasps the essence of the *kōan* or not is determined freely by the interrelation between the qualities of the disciple and the ability of the Master; mutual understanding or the congenial temper of both plays an important role in this matter.

Examining some old and famous examples of *kōan* used in the *Zen* sect may clarify the content and nature of these seemingly baffling word problems. Some representatives from the many are the *kōan* of Tōzan's *ma-sangin* (the 3.7 lb. of flax-seed oil) and that of Jōshū's *u-mu* (*being and non-being*). The history of the former is as follows. A certain monk asked Tōzan-Ryōkai, the *Zen* master, 'What is the Buddha?' He gave him this answer, 'The Buddha is *ma-sangin*.' Based on this episode, many masters used to order their disciples to reflect on and clarify the true meaning of this answer. If we judge Tōzan's answer as off the mark, saying we cannot induce any meaning from such irrationality, we are not able to pass through the *kōan*. That is not the way of *kufū* in *Zen*. The Master's absurd answer is used to make his disciple do *kufū* and realize the inexpressible true spirit of the Buddha Way. We cannot find any logical reason for why Tōzan's answer must be what it is. He might well have given any answer for it; he happened to answer thus at that time. The disciple, who was told to clarify the meaning of Tōzan's answer, could not have thought it out with his rational faculty. Even if he had been able to express a reasonable answer, he could not have passed this *kōan*. Rather, if he returned an unexpected reply and showed purport beyond words, even if it was absurd, he might have passed through it. *Zen mondō* (*Zen* dialogues) are of such nature.

Jōshū's *kōan*, *u-mu* is similar. The history of it is as follows. A certain monk asked Jōshū-Jūshin, the *Zen* Master, 'Is there Buddha-nature in a dog?' Jōshū answered 'Yes'. But when another monk asked him the same question at another time, he answered 'No'. The aim of this *kōan* is, as in the case of the former, to let one reflect and clarify the true Way of Buddha through contradictory answers. In this case too, even if one were able to have reasoned an answer out, he would not be given permission to pass. The fact is that Jūshin himself explained to each monk why he answered him as he did. But any correct answer is not always necessary for the training of a monk, who ought to express what he truly feels through his own experience and practice. The truth could be proven by a tacit understanding between a Master and his disciple.

Such a peculiar mode of representing the experience of *zazen* practice is highly significant. It is especially useful for conventional Buddhism, because it clears it of the formalism of *kyōshū*. But a danger is that *kōan* practice will also go astray if it becomes formalized. Such a way of understanding is lacking in objective validity because of its very individuality. If a tacit or telepathic understanding between a Master and a disciple has a decisive weight in judging whether one passes a *kōan*, the mastering of the technique of how to find the way to the Master's heart served a disciple as an important aid. Some disciples who were ingenious in such techniques passed their *kōan* in quick succession and boasted of the numbers of *kōan* passed. They were too eager to obtain sanction of the attainment of the Way, and to occupy a higher position in the hierarchy of the priesthood without endeavouring to get to true self-advancement. There arose the tendency to bring the individuality of the *kōan* even into their daily lives and to show off playful or eccentric behaviour there, too. The corruption of religious practice, which should have been avoided, the vices of the *Zen* sect of Buddhism, became more and more conspicuous.

Such a corruption of *Zen* was caused by overattention to the *kōan*, just as the followers of the *kyōshū* paid too much attention to the annotation of the Scriptures. They deviated from right discipline by erroneously thinking that they could get *shōka* (enlightenment as the result of *zazen* practice) through passing many *kōan* and arriving at higher stages in the priestly hierarchy. Moreover they thought that they no longer needed to practise once they had got *shōka*. Soon this mistaken method comparable with going up the stairs in order to get *shōka* became despised as *hashigo-Zen* (*hashigo* means a ladder) and practices which aimed only at attaining *shōka* became despised as *taigo-Zen* (*taigo* means 'to do nothing but to wait for enlightenment'). Such a tendency came about because some people thought *kōan* were absolutely indispensable to the practice of *Zen*. Because of this, another form of *Zen, mokushō-Zen* (meditation-*Zen*) arose which rejected the conventional *Zen* of *kōan-Zen. Mokushō-Zen* did not always belittle the *kufū* of the *kōan* but it did not regard it as everything. It adopted *zazen* as a basic principle through which we should find our true self by ourselves. *Shikan-taza* may be regarded as being counter to *kōan-Zen* in this sense. *Sōtō* Buddhism which Dōgen brought back with him from China is a school based on *mokushō-Zen*. When he came across this kind of *Zen* in China, he realized that this was the true Way which he would follow throughout his life. Dōgen's *genjō-kōan* can only be comprehended when this historical background regarding the development of *kōan-Zen* (also known as *kanna-Zen*) is given adequate attention.

3 Dōgen's view of kōan, and the meaning of genjō

Dōgen practised *kyōshū* when he first entered the priesthood. Soon he became dissatisfied with *kyōshū* and entered the *Zen* sect, which was that of *kōan-Zen*. He was not content with this either. He happened to come across *mokushō-Zen* in China and found in it the true Way. *Mokushō-Zen* does not always disregard the *kōan*, but its primary characteristic is the practice of *zazen*. If *mokushō-Zen* attached too much importance to the *kōan*, it would fall into the so-called 'vices of *Zen*'. But, on the contrary, if it ignored the *kōan* wholly, it could only achieve a mediocre result in following the Buddha Way. Ultimately, it depends upon the Master's discernment as to how to regard the *kōan* and how to deal with it.

Generally, *kōan* are derived from old moral sayings such as the *kosoku-kōan* (the old *kōan*) which originated in *Zen mondō*. The number of *kōan* increased through the ages. Their number, however, was limited. If we again select from among them some appropriate examples for *kufū*, the numbers would be limited even more. For example, Daie-Shūkō, a representative *Zen* Master of *kōan-Zen*, advises us to do *kufū* on only Jōshū's *kōan, u-mu*, especially the *mu kōan*. This is one approach; Dōgen took another. He permitted unlimited numbers of *kōan*. Why was the number of *kōan* not limited by Dōgen? The reason may be summed up in the following three points. First, as in the case of other Masters, he took up the actions of the Patriarchs as *kōan*. Many of them appear in the *Shōbōgenzō*. Second, he adopted sayings from the Buddhist Scriptures. Of course they had already been picked out and compiled as *kosoku-kōan*, but their numbers were limited; only a few associated with *Zen* were selected. Dōgen suggested that *kōan* should be chosen from throughout the Scriptures. In fact, many of them are treated in the *Shōbōgenzō*. This is natural, because if the actions of the Patriarchs are to be taken for models, it is absurd to suggest a valid reason for excluding from *kōan* the precepts of the Buddha himself. A difference lies only in each Master's way of making a model of them. Dōgen using his excellent discretion selected many *kōan* from the Scriptures for his *Shōbōgenzō*. Third, Dōgen chose *kōan* not only from the Scriptures, but also selected them widely from Nature at large. For example, in the chapter, *Kobutsu-Shin (The Mind of the Ancient, Excellent Patriarchs)* in the *Shōbōgenzō*, Dōgen says, 'In spring, all trees and grasses begin to sprout and bloom. All of these are a speaking and questioning of the *kobutsu*.' The speaking and questioning of the old, excellent Patriarchs are nothing but *kōan*.

If the words of the old Patriarchs through which we do *kufū* are *kōan*, all things in Nature, which are the expressions of the old Patriarchs themselves, must necesarily be *kōan*. The quotation above is from Dōgen's reference to the dialogue between Nan'yō-Echū, a Chinese *Zen* Master who died in AD 775, and a certain monk. The monk asked the Master: 'What is *kobutsu-shin*?' Nanyō replied: 'Fence, wall, tile, stones.' Commenting on this dialogue, Dōgen suggests that we can hear the words of the old Patriarchs in every tree and leaf of grass, and that everything in this world, including fences, walls, tiles, and stones, should be *kōan*.

Dōgen acknowledges *kōan* as being in all objects in the universe. A similar assertion can be seen in other places of the *Shōbōgenzō*. In the last paragraph of the chapter, *Keisei-Sanshoku (Sounds of the Valley-Streams and Colours of the Mountains)*, we find the following passage: 'If you practise correctly, the sounds and colours of valley-streams and mountains will never hold back their 84,000 hymns of praise and their teaching of the Way toward Buddha.' Again in the first paragraph of the chapter, *Sansui-Kyō (The Mountain and River Sutra)*, we read: 'The mountains and rivers before us actualize the Way of the ancient Buddhas.' '*Keisei-sanshoku*' or '84,000 hymns of praise', these words are from some Chinese *Zen* Buddhist layman, and the problems treated in *Sansui-Kyō* are found in certain Chinese *Zen* texts. But Dōgen's genius for recognizing *kōan* in the natural world is quite original. What is preached in *Sansui-Kyō* harmonizes very well with the Japanese sensitivity to the natural environment. If everything which presents itself to us is a *kōan*, the *genjō-kōan* undoubtedly proclaims the truth that actuality is instruction.

As we have seen, Dōgen's *genjō-kōan* is in sharp contrast to conventional *kōan-Zen* in the respect that it recognizes *kōan* in all things. But, there are some points to be considered in connection with this matter. The first point is how Dōgen's *kōan* is associated with the essential spirit of Buddhism. If it has nothing to do with the precepts of Buddhism, it is heretical in nature, though it is original to Dōgen. We must know here that Dōgen's preaching has a direct connection with the essential spirit of Mahayana Buddhism. Mahayana Buddhism, which is constructed elaborately along the lines of the original preaching of the Buddha, adopts a broad interpretation of it. It is said that Mahayana Buddhism's basic spirit is expressed in *shohō-jissō*. *Shohō-jissō* is the concept that all things (*shohō*) are themselves what truth should be (*jissō*), that is to say, *the Way involved in the world of the Buddha* (*jissō*). To put it in another way, it means all things that show themselves to us will lead us to enlightenment, and this way of thinking is equivalent in meaning to that of the *genjō-kōan*. This explains why the *genjō-kōan* has, for a long time, been said to be another name for *shohō-jissō*. In this sense, Dōgen's *genjō-kōan* has a close connection with the traditional character of Buddhism. We may safely say that Dōgen has developed the essential spirit of Buddhism to its fullest potential with his teaching on the *genjō-kōan*.

The second point to be considered is that the *genjō-kōan* is free from any fixed idea, freer than the limited, conventional *kosoku-kōan*. This freedom of *genjō-kōan* is a logical consequence of its essential nature; it regards all the actualizations in this world as *kōan*. But this does not imply an arbitrary quality. The *Zen* practitioner understands that he/she should select and actualize the real and absolute Way revealed to us in the unlimited realities of this world. If *zazen* is the practice through which we return to absolute nothingness, the *genjō-kōan* teaches us the freedom with which we should return to our original point so that we can start again from it. This is one of the unique theories of Dōgen, developed in the *Shōbōgenzō*.

The third point, which is inseparably related to the above, is that the *genjō-kōan* is the *kōan* which should be engendered in us by our personal realization. The numberless objective realities, which have the possibility of becoming *kōan*, will not turn into true *kōan* until they are actualized as *kōan* in us. This is because objective realities are neutral and transform themselves in response to the attitude of the subjective viewer. For example, peach blossoms in full bloom show various aspects in response to each observer; to a painter, they may be the subject of a painting, to an orchardman the coming fruits of his work, to a merchant the objects of trade, and to some other person enjoyable objects for appreciation. It depends upon the attitude, upon the mind which observes whether they can turn into *kōan* or not; one cannot be a *Zen* Master until objective reality is actualized as *kōan* by the viewer.

There was a *Zen* Master called Reiun-Shigon, who grasped the Way at the sight of some peach blossoms in full bloom. Dōgen takes pleasure in quoting his actions as an example. He refers to it in the chapter, *Bukkyō (The Buddhist Sutra)*, in the *Shōbōgenzō*, adding as follows, 'a Sutra, as it is called, is all the ten quarters of the world. No time and place will be without its being a Sutra.' In short, Reiun, who viewed the peach blossoms in the light that all the ten quarters of the world should be Sutra, obtained spiritual enlightenment by actualizing the *kōan*. The peach blossoms in front of him were not only *kōan* for him, but he himself had actualized them as *kōan*. The peach blossoms could never be *kōan* for anyone, but for Reiun; they were to be *kōan* for him.

Each person grasps spiritual enlightenment through different *kōan*, and in most cases some accident works as a *kōan*. The case above, generally known as 'the cause of Reiun's spiritual enlightenment through peach blossoms' is one example. Another equally famous one is known as *kyōgen-kyakuchiku*. When a *Zen* Master called Kyōgen-Shikan (?AD 898) was sweeping a garden, a small stone happened to hit one of the bamboo trees, making a sound. He experienced spiritual enlightenment by hearing it. In other words, *kyakuchiku* (hitting the bamboo tree) worked as a *kōan* for him, or he actualized it as a *kōan*. We may say it happened to be a *kōan* because he actualized it as a *kōan*. All the phenomenal things of the world before us are *kōan* because we are able to actualize them as *kōan* and because this fact has been proven by the various actions of the most eminent *Zen* Masters of the past. *Kosoku-kōan* is of the same nature. If someone were ordered to do *kufū* on Jōshū's *mu* as a *kōan* and attained spiritual enlightenment by chance after many years of hard practice, he would be given the sanction of a great *satori*. In this case, the *mu* actualized itself as a *kōan* through his great *satori*. If the person failed to attain *satori*, it would only be that the *mu* could not turn into a *kōan* for him. As in the case of this *kosoku-kōan*, a *kōan* is only a prepared possibility.

Dōgen thinks that countless possible *kōan* exist in the human world as well as in the natural world. Indeed, this should be so. One could possibly experience spiritual enlightenment by chance through anything, at any time, even if the actualization of Jōshū's *Zen kōan* were impossible. The Buddha himself achieved spiritual awakening through Nature at large, and never advised his followers to attain *satori* through special or limited *kōan*. The significance of Dōgen's *kōan* teaching is that it freed *Zen* Buddhism from a narrow and restricted *kōan-Zen*, opening the freer way of *satori* through one's own will. Dōgen taught that, 'If we do *zazen* for a long time, we shall suddenly grasp the Way and realize that *zazen* is the right way of Buddhism.' Again he teaches, 'By virtue of a long and patient practice in the Way, the enlightenment will dawn upon our mind.' That is to say, it depends upon the mental attitude of each man as to what he can actualize as *kōan*. He may unexpectedly grasp an opportunity to discover the Way to *satori*, if he keeps up his efforts to practise *zazen* and to do *kufū* according to his own ability.

By way of a summary it is well to note that the *genjō-kōan* should be grasped essentially in the meaning that 'actuality is instruction' but at the same time, it requires practical effort according to the meaning of 'actualizing instruction'. When one actualizes a *kōan*, the *kōan* will realize for us what it is to be, and by realizing it, the *kōan* will be able to be called 'real *kōan*'. 'To be' (the existence of *kōan*) turns into 'to become' (the actualization of it) by 'doing' (practice). The *Shōbōgenzō* constantly reiterates the truth that a '*kōan* should be actualized through the effort of each one of us.' This is the most important point to be considered regarding the problem of the *kōan*. To actualize *kōan* is of the essence of *zazen* practice.

4 Genjō and the three gō or karma

The centrality of actualizing the *genjō-kōan* was discussed in the preceding section. This practice must be understood in three phases, because practice is deed and in Buddhism deed is generally grasped as the three *gō* (karmas). *Gō* in Buddhism is a term expressing the reality that each of one's deeds inevitably invites a retribution in proportion to its quality; a present deed should also be considered as the retributive consequence of a past one. *Gō* traditionally consists of three phases: *shin-gō, ku-gō*, and *i-gō*. *Shin-gō* is the *gō* manifested by a deed, *ku-gō* that of speech, and *i-gō* the *gō* of thought. These three *gō* have an effect upon both oneself and others, by mere words and thoughts without any direct physical action. The essence of the practical ethics of the *genjō-kōan* can be classified through examining these three phases of *gō*.

Of the three, *shin-gō* should be counted foremost, because it manifests itself as a clear and definite phase in actual deeds. Dōgen elaborates on this phase in the chapter on the *Genjō-kōan* in the *Shōbōgenzō*. It can be found in the paragraph where Dōgen preaches about the significance of the practical embodiment of the Buddha Way in us using the allegory of the living way of fish and birds: 'Fish in the water and birds in the sky, finding the water and the sky to be places for peaceful living rest their whole lives. The realization of such an experience on a personal, human level might be called *genjō-kōan*.' That is to say, the true meaning of the *genjō-kōan* is that one should actualize the truth of the Buddhist dharma as *kōan* according to one's own practice; the *kōan* is presented in its various forms to this world, so one should practise by doing *kufū* and embody the truth in himself through his own practical experience. In this way one can attain a similar realization of peaceful living and pleasurable work. Such is the realization of the *genjō-kōan* by *shin-gō*.

The chapter, *Mujō-Seppō (The Precept of Non-Sentient Being)* in the *Shōbōgenzō* gives us suggestions about the relationship between the *genjō-kōan* and *ku-gō*. In the opening paragraph, we read: 'That a preaching preaches a preaching means *genjō-kōan* conveying a dharma from Patriarch to Patriarch.' The chapter, *Mujō-Seppō* deals with the idea in Buddhism that *mujō* (non-sentient beings like mountains, grasses, and trees) are able to preach (*seppō*). This idea may be construed logically from the thought mentioned already in the preceding explanation that '84,000 hymns of praise come from the valley-streams and mountains.' However if *mujō* can preach, how can we hear it? Probably we may not. This question is at the crux of the dilemma of what to do about *kufū* as *kōan*. To this question Dōgen answers, 'If you are not willing to hear, the loudest voices could not reach your ears; if you are willing to hear, even the silent voices could reach your ears.' Indeed, those who are not ready to listen or have not sufficient spiritual faculties to listen would be deaf to any earnest preaching.

On the other hand, those who are ready to listen and are in the right state to hear can understand even the implications of the precepts. In some cases, they hear unspoken words 'spoken' by the mere expressions of a speaker. There is, after all, no difference to the ear between the precepts of the Patriarch as a living, human being and those of the valleys and mountains as non-sentient beings, so long as they reach the ear. To put it in another way, 'a dharma preaches a dharma'; whatever may preach, sentient beings (*ujō*) or valleys and mountains, a dharma is a dharma to the ear. The only question is whether one is ready to hear or not. This brings us to Dōgen's opening paragraph that 'a preaching preaches a preaching', an argument drawn from the viewpoint that various Buddhas and Patriarchs, in reality, were practising *mujō-seppō*.

In such a theoretical context as the above, Dōgen opened the chapter of *Mujō-Seppō* with the sentence 'a preaching preaches a preaching means *genjō-kōan* conveying a dharma from Patriarch to Patriarch.' This means also that the *genjō-kōan* contains a phase which can preach a dharma in speech, that is to say, a phase to actualize a *kōan* as *ku-gō*. And the fact that the true dharma can be preached in speech must explain the fundamental reason why *kōan* can be actualized by speech. What Dōgen explores in the opening paragraph is one way of actualizing *kōan*, that of a Patriarch conveying a dharma to a Patriarch. It stands to reason that when one comprehends a dharma through personal experience, one will be able to speak of it; if one cannot, one will not be able to preach a dharma nor convey it to future generations. What can be spoken must also be able to be expressed in written words. In a broad sense, *gō* in the written word may well be called *ku-gō*. Viewed in this light, the *Shōbōgenzō* can be regarded as Dōgen's actualization of the great *kōan* through *ku-gō*.

Third, a pertinent suggestion regarding the actualization of the *kōan* as *i-gō* is offered in the chapter, *Kūge* (*The Flower of Emptiness*), in the *Shōbōgenzō*. The conclusion of the argument in it is that 'the way of truth is like a flower in the sky, and cannot be grasped by our ordinary senses.' Dōgen explores the truth that 'the true nature of communication from mind to mind' (*ishin-denshin*) between Shakyamuni and Kashō, one of his disciples, is a *kōan* which actualizes a kind of supersensible world, just as 'blurred eyes' mean paradoxically the mind's eye with which a holy man can grasp truth, though it is seen only with 'blurred eyes' by men of mediocrity. A holy man sees *kūge*, which paradoxically means the brilliant flower of truth though it is seen as the flower of emptiness to men of mediocrity. Dōgen expresses the reality that a *kōan* can be actualized in certain minds, which suggests nothing but the truth about *i-gō* as an inner work. The importance of *i-gō* should not be overlooked; all the more because the historical fact of this great concept of *ishin-denshin* has been thought to be the origin of *Zen* Buddhism. One ought not to forget that all actions have their motives in our minds.

Dōgen carefully, and with great clarity explored the varied aspects of the *genjō-kōan* as that which is meant to actualize a *kōan* through the three *gō* of thought, speech and deed. If the distinctive character of the *genjō-kōan* is considered at all, what emerges is its place in the practical ethics of Dōgen. To practise actually or to know through physical experience is the essential character of Dōgen's precepts. When speaking of practice, without a doubt, *zazen* is meant first of all. This may be supported by the fact that Dōgen's precepts have been preached with *shikan-taza* as a normative force. Embodiment of the true spirit of the Buddha is attainable through the practice of *zazen*. In other words, *zazen* is the practice for embodying the true spirit of the Buddha in ourselves. Thus the practice has a definite aim. In order to fulfil that aim, other disciplines must accompany *zazen*. The other disciplines also depend on practice. Such an interlocking philosophical system with its all inclusiveness is a testament to the creative genius of Dōgen as a *Zen* Master. The striking feature of Dōgen's practical philosophy is that it is not limited to dharma but covers the laws of general society, just as he did not limit the scope of the *kōan* to the field of *kosoku-kōan*, but extended it to Nature at large.

Chapter 3

Practice

1 Shiaku-shuzen (the practice of doing good and refraining from doing evil)

The Master under whom Dōgen studied *Sōtō Zen* was Tendō Nyojō, an excellent monk of high rank who lived in China. Dōgen spent the first half of his four years in China knocking on the gates of many masters' residences only to fail in finding a true one whose pupil he wished to become. That was until he came across Nyojō. From then on he became an ardent disciple of this Master. Dōgen records the experiences of this apprenticeship to Nyojō in *Hōkyō-ki*, which consists mainly of the dialogues between the two. In one of those dialogues the Master proclaims: 'We must not arbitrarily call the true Dharma, which we inherit and hand down, the *Zen* sect. I am the only supervisor of the Buddha-Dharma. All other schools belong to Patriarchs.'

Dōgen accepted and followed this view of the Master faithfully, trying to avoid using the term, *Zen* sect, in the *Shōbōgenzō* as much as possible. Such a dogmatic way of thinking is apt to be quite common in the founder of a religious sect. It is natural that the originator of a sect should regard his own viewpoint as infallible and absolute. Of course, this is certainly untenable in the objective light of formal research. Although Dōgen uses the phrases 'our Dharma' or 'the orthodox Dharma' instead of *Zen* sect, the distinction is not valid. Even if he professes himself to be the only orthodox supervisor of the Buddha Dharma, it is a claim subject to close scrutiny and subsequent disagreement. On the other hand, an examination of the entire structure of Dōgen's precepts does support Dōgen's claim, because the total system is of such a nature as to expound faithfully the basic spirit of Buddhism, while taking into account every aspect of it.

20

This argument is proven especially by the *Shōbōgenzō*, a work which draws its basic doctrinal structure from the precepts of Nyojō. When careful attention is given to Dōgen's comprehensive view, we cannot but admit that he is worthy to be called the orthodox supervisor of the true Dharma. As a corollary to his system, Dōgen holds that *kōan* should not be limited to *kosoku-kōan* but extended to the world of the Buddhist Scriptures and to Nature at large. This view presents a great contrast to the narrow approaches of the other sects. What lay at the centre of Dōgen's 'way' was a return to the original standpoint of Buddha himself, which in turn necessitated accepting literally the Scriptures of the Buddha as they had historically developed. This approach was obviously quite reactionary at that time, the thirteenth century, in Japan's religious history.

The contents of the *Shōbōgenzō* are diverse. They convey to the reader the impression that Dōgen has given a distinctly personal view to the general outline of the body and substance of Buddhism. If we try to systematize the contents so as to approach them with ease, various modes of organization can be imagined, but this only makes the work more mazelike and complicated. So avoiding such a quandary, we are going instead to inquire only into those phases of the *Shōbōgenzō* which have universal meaning for our own time. It seems, therefore, natural to attempt this inquiry through the practical elements found in Dōgen's precepts.

There is a paragraph in the *Shōbōgenzō-zuimon-ki* (*The First Hand Record of the Master's Precept by the Follower sitting beside him*) in which Dōgen seems to lay stress on the practice of what is being taught. This work is an account of Dōgen's follower, Ejō. Therefore it is less reliable as material for academic study than the manuscripts written by the Master himself. But, may not truth often be uttered casually in the unguided and familiar conversations which are a part of every day life? In this sense, Ejō's record is no less reliable, especially when we remember that Ejō was the Dharma-successor to Dōgen's philosophy, and always attended on him. The following paragraphs from the work clarify Dōgen's attitude towards the practice of his teachings.

It is very much an error for *Zen* monks to do evil under the pretext that they need not do good nor accumulate virtuous deeds. I have never heard of any old commandment which said that monks should love evil. Tanka Tennen the *Zen* Master burned a wooden Buddha-image. It may seem evil but it is one way to show the truth of the Dharma. According to the record of his life, he was always cordial in sitting or standing as if before a guest of honor. Even in sitting for some time, he used to sit cross-legged and in standing, to clasp his hands palm to palm. He held the requisites of daily life in the temple precincts as dear to him as his own eyes, valuing good things, however small and never failing to praise the monks for their diligence in the Way. He was especially exemplary in the conduct of his daily life. So his deeds as written down prove that even now he is an example of observance for those in *Zen* monasteries.

Along with him, all praiseworthy *Zen* masters and enlightened Patriarchs, it is said, observed the austerities and led solemn lives, making much of seemingly little things. I have never heard of enlightened priests who neglected good deeds.

Therefore, if the novices try to follow the Way of the Patriarchs they should not belittle their good actions. In devoting themselves to the Way of Buddhism, the great Way practiced by the Buddhas and Patriarchs, they will never fail to bring together many kinds of good. Now that we have fully realized that all laws are manifestations of the Buddha Way, we must grasp evil as evil, and therefore far from the Way of the Buddhas and Patriarchs; good on the contrary is decidedly good and integrally connected with the Way. If this is so, how is it possible, then, that the world of *sanbō* (the Buddha, the Dharma and a priest) is not to be respected?

The gist of these passages is to be seen in the following remark: 'therefore, if the novices try to follow the Way of the Patriarchs they should not belittle their good actions.' The Japanese equivalent for 'good actions' is *zen-gon*. In this case, *zen-gon* is, in other words, 'good-*karma*', for *gon* (or *kon*) connotes *gō* or *karma*. *Gon* etymologically means root, that is to say, it suggests a source or reservoir of energy, from which retributions are begotten according to the kinds of actions one chooses. The true meaning of this succinct summary is, therefore, that in order to follow the Way of the Buddha, one must never fail to make good *karma*. After clarifying this point, Dōgen states that our faith in the Way of Buddhism should be unshakable; he stresses that the practice of the principles that the Patriarchs have advocated, necessarily means that good is done. All the laws therefore of moral rectitude are related to Buddhism. Based on such a view, he draws this conclusion: 'we must grasp evil as definitely evil and therefore far from the Way of the Buddhas and Patriarchs; *Good* on the contrary is decidedly *good* and integrally connected with the Way.' This requires of Buddhists a determined attitude to reject *evil* and to do *good*. The practical morality of Dōgen's precepts is very profound in this respect.

There are some further points to be considered in relation to the above excerpt from Dōgen's teaching. First, take notice of the opening two sentences:

> It is very much an error for *Zen* monks to do evil under the pretext that they need not do good nor accumulate virtuous deeds. I have never heard of any old commandment which said that monks should love evil.

From these statements we can hazard a guess that in Dōgen's time some *Zen* monks did not hesitate to do evil, excusing themselves by the rationalization that neither good deeds nor virtue were required of them. Dōgen himself in the *Shōbōgenzō* records that he witnessed such degenerate tendencies in Buddhism while living in China during the Sun Dynasty. Perhaps such laxity was not a phenomenon of that time only. With the increased prosperity of *Zen*, such deviant behaviour increased and has had a wide-spread influence down through the ages. As we have seen already, it is possible for *Zen* to deviate from the truth of the Dharma, because *Zen* can be mistakenly identified with mere *zazen* practice. One is apt to think he has mastered *Zen* if only he can do *kufū* and pass some of the *kōans*, thereby displaying the outer wrappings of the *Zen* Way without any regard for the inner spirit of the Scriptures. One cannot attain to the true Buddha Way in such a manner. The *kōan* should be regarded as integrally bound up with the Dharma which supports it. All true *Zen* Masters have practised *zazen* according to this principle, but minor monks are apt to fall into error because of a spiritual near-sightedness which leads to stressing trivialities.

The following seems to provide Dōgen's view of the problem: 'Tanka Tennen the *Zen* Master burned a wooden Buddha-image. It may seem evil but it is one way to show the truth of the Dharma.' This is told in reference to the historical fact that Tanka Tennen happened to meet an old friend on a cold winter day and burned a Buddha image made of wood so that they might warm themselves by a fire. Dōgen suggests that the same manner imitated by a monk should be subjected to criticism but, in the case of Tanka Tennen it can be forgiven, because he provided us with the excellent lesson that we should not adhere to form at the expense of the true meaning of the Buddha. Dōgen reiterates the point that we should not judge a man by his overt action but, by the totality of his character which includes its expression by his daily behaviour. The apt phrase 'according to the record of his life' which follows the above example links the action of the moment with the constancy of a well-formed follower of the Buddha. Dōgen continues to say that other virtuous Masters and enlightened Patriarchs were of the same mind in such matters, stressing that real *Zen* practice ought to be accompanied by the manifestation of good deeds.

It is not Dōgen's merely fanciful idea that *Zen* ought to be accompanied by good deeds. If *Zen* is one of the Ways of Buddha, it ought to be natural that 'one should do good, and refrain from doing evil.' This central tenet of *shiaku-shuzen* is then the true essence of Buddhism. The following *Shichi-Butsu-tsūkai-ge* (*The Hymn of the Commandments preached unanimously by the Seven ancient Buddhas in addition to Shakyamuni*) shows us such a purpose.

> *Shoaku-makusa* (Do no evil.)
> *Shuzen-bugyō* (Practise with sincerity all that is good.)
> *Jijō-goi* (And naturally your mind will purify itself.)
> *Zesho-bukkyō* (These are the teachings of various Buddhas.)

This hymn has been accepted traditionally as the answer to the question 'What is Buddhism?' Dōgen gives special attention to this problem in the chapter, *Shoaku-Makusa* of the *Shōbōgenzō* and develops it into a highly formulated theory. Buddhism would lose its truth, he argues, if *shiaku-shuzen* were not emphasized as its essential precept. *Shikan-taza*, if it had nothing to do with the deeds of good and evil, would become a ritual *zazen* not a part of Buddhism but only a type of mental exercise. Of course *zazen* as a way of controlling and heightening as well as transcending the mental faculties is not categorically denied, but without ethical underpinning it is incomplete. For example, if while practising *zazen* something immoral is cultivated by the mind, an undefined anxiety or guilt follows, so that the sitter can neither experience any spiritual unity and stability, nor concentrate his/her energy upon anything. *Zazen* practice as Buddhism will never attain to its completeness if it is not accompanied by *shiaku-shuzen*. It is essential to grasp the reason why Dōgen advocates *shikan-taza* while he lays special emphasis on *shiaku-shuzen*. Only in this way will a fundamental approach to his teaching be possible.

2 The standard of good and evil and the problem of transcendence

As seen so far, *shiaku-shuzen* is one special characteristic of Buddhism. But there are some problems to be considered in connection with this matter. The first question is that of a standard by which we should decide what is good and conversely what is evil. Dōgen found it difficult to decide such a problem absolutely with only public morality as a norm and ended up saying, that 'the standard of good and evil is undefinable.' This seems to be very reasonable and true. But, on the other hand, the standard should not be an arbitrary one dependent only on personal preference. It requires for its formulation a wide knowledge about various teachings and deep reflection on their myriad facets. Putting forth such a view, Dōgen reaches this conclusion: 'one should discriminate carefully, practising true good and giving up true evil.'

Such basic questions about good and evil, their manifestations, and the norms for moral choice have been repeatedly discussed as traditional, ethical problems. Nevertheless we have not been able to reach a definite conclusion as yet, though we have tentative ones varying from case to case. Moreover since such a discussion should be confined primarily to ethics *per se* or to philosophy, Buddhism would not go deep into the ramifications of this question. This is partly because Buddhism does not consider the formulation of definite answers to such problems as a part of Buddhism and also partly because it fears that such discussion is apt to become mere toying with ideas or discussion for discussion's sake. Buddhism has discarded such useless discussion by calling it *keron* (idle discussion). Laying aside the problem of *keron*, Dōgen seems to insist that there is no way to judge good and evil except according to one's own discernment, which involves consulting and weighing the various opinions and moral teachings of others.

Furthermore Dōgen says, 'A man's mind is not inherently good or bad. Moral discretion depends upon circumstances and occasions.' According to Dōgen, good and evil depend upon a given situation so that even if we repeat the same thing, it will become good or evil according to the situation. Man's mind is not predetermined as good or evil. Dōgen states conclusively that: 'good circumstances will urge us to do good, while bad ones urge us to do evil. We must not regard our mind as primarily evil. We must only try to be led by good circumstances and occasions.' This statement appears to be a devious theory which shifts the source of responsibility onto conditions or circumstances, while disregarding the inner disposition of the individual. But it is not. The responsibility lies nowhere but in oneself, not in the outer world. The reason is because it is we, ourselves, who respond to situations, whether they are good or bad. As to this problem, we must reflect that it is by our own discernment that we pass judgment about ourselves as agents of good and evil. Discernment informed by wisdom and knowledge together with the sifting of ideas concerning ethical behaviour will bring us to the actual deed. So what is asked is that we endeavour to cultivate that wisdom and knowledge which heightens discernment. Such an approach in turn explains why Dōgen stresses continuous intellectual as well as mental discipline.

The second question to be considered is that of whether everyone can consistently and faithfully observe Dōgen's teaching that we should do good only and do it thoroughly. There were some founders of religious sects, who exerted themselves to the utmost to do good in everything, but they found it beyond their powers. Finally they discovered a mode of salvation in a Way which urges them to throw themselves on the compassion of the Buddha. Sects such as *Jōdo-mon* – *Jōdo-shū, Ji-shū, Shin-shū* – are of this nature. Here, to be sure, is one possible choice. The founders of these sects must have had the faculty for seeing into the heart of the matter, of grasping that men cannot possibly attain to perfect goodness. With this clear vision, they were able to open the Way toward the Buddha Dharma. But Dōgen takes another Way. He is no less a believer in the compassion of the Buddha, yet he would not abandon himself to it, but chooses to study it. Not only does he study compassion, which is a major facet of the Buddha, but also tries to embody the whole of the Buddha in himself. Needless to say, the Buddha is absolute and unlimited in His compassion, wisdom and virtue. He is forever beyond our desperate and continuous efforts to reach Him. Dōgen's advice is to: 'nevertheless, make a determined effort towards such attainment.' This is not merely a rash idea of Dōgen's. It has its own foundation in *Bosatsu-dō* (the Way of *Bodhisattva*). The *Bosatsu-dō* is the Way of Mahayana Buddhism by which one realizes the true spirit of Shakyamuni in a highly idealized form; Hinayana Buddhism, on the other hand, goes no further than an imitation of His apparent actions and teachings. In *Bosatsu-dō* one forever makes an effort towards this ideal even though it involves endless transmigrations of birth and death. Possibly, we might not realize or attain to it in one life, but the result of such effort is never wasted. It amounts to *shakku-ruitoku* (the accumulation of virtue), with which we will be able to get nearer to the ideal step by step even in our numerous lives after death.

Although having chosen the Way of *Bosatsu*, sometimes we may be attacked by the anxiety that we may slide into sin against our will because of numerous faults and weaknesses. Or, we are pursued by a guilty obsession with the past, so that we may not take a single step forward along the Way. Dōgen suggests that the way of repentance is the remedy for such anxiety. Such a suggestion is found in several places in the *Shōbōgenzō*, especially in the chapter, *Keisei-Sanshoku*: 'If you are physically or mentally lazy and lack faith, you must repent toward the Buddha and show your earnest resolve. The virtue of repentance will save us and purifies the mind.' Beginning with this statement, Dōgen goes on to discuss the significance of repentance with great enthusiasm. If such a moderate way of salvation is available to us, anyone of us should be able to walk the way of *shiaku-shuzen* without scruples. This way is not only necessary for Buddhists, but also for everyone who wants to attain peace in the world.

The third question to be considered in this discussion is that of the practice of *mu-ga* (selflessness). The most characteristic principle which determines the Way of Buddhism is the concept of *shohō-muga*, namely that all forms of existence do not have the right to possess individual existences themselves as a prerogative. Dōgen's practical ethics originates in this very concept. With the denial of *ga-ken* (self-centredness) or *go-ga* (self-attachment), Dōgen impresses upon us the necessity of freedom from *ga-shū*, clinging to a fixed, egoistic 'mind'. Dōgen expounds the following in the *Shōbōgenzō-zuimon-ki*:

> The primary requisite for the followers of Buddha is to leave self-centredness. This means we must not be attached to our body. Even if we have mastered the sayings of ancient persons, have always done *zazen* and our mind is as steadfast as iron or stone, yet we shall find it impossible to master the Way of the Buddhas or Patriarchs, even in long *kalpas* of repeated birth and death, as long as we are attached to ourselves.

In this statement, Dōgen teaches us that freedom from *ga-shū* is the most important state for the followers of Buddhism to attain to, and those who are not ready for the effort will not be able to master the Way, even if they practise *zazen* with fixed determination. Having determined therefore that *shohō-muga* is the fundamental principle of Buddhism, Dōgen's precept is not inconsistent. The truth inherent in the words 'freedom from *ga-shū*' is negated if we do not first have the realization of *shohō-muga*. Nevertheless, the Patriarch argues, the former may be accepted independently of the latter. According to Buddhism, all things flow and nothing is permanent. This is called *shogyō-mujō*. So if we incorrectly perceive such an inconstant world which is forever in flux as stationary, and our individual self as fixed within it, we are inevitably led to a distorted understanding or judgment. For this reason Buddhism exhorts us to open our eyes to the truth of *shohō-muga* so that we may acquire 'absolute and true peace of mind'. In short, what is being described is *nehan-jakujō* (emancipation in Nirvana). *Nehan-jakujō* in Buddhism is related therefore to concepts of *shohō-muga* and *shogyō-mujō*, with the latter informing the total character of such emancipation.

Shohō-muga does not degenerate into nihilism, even if it regards all existence as incapable of possessing the true self. Rather, because of the annihilation of the self, we are able to get ready to fit into the flux of all 'that which changes'. *Shohō-muga* teaches such a fundamental attitude of mind towards the living things of the world. One further complication which suggests itself is that in order to grasp the various aspects of these elusive realities, we cannot but fix them into some unchangeable pattern. Only by fixing them, are we able to grasp them, and at the same time make a comparison with other realities. Buddhism does not go into the matter of denying such a human process at length, but regards it merely as an expedient though not inevitable means. Buddhism claims that reality does not have any fixed entity. Consequently Dōgen taught that any practical ethic, if it existed as Buddhism, should be considered in relation to this idea of *muga*.

Pursuing the point further introduces two related concepts. The phrase, *gashū-ridatsu* (freedom from the fixed egoistic mind), contains the religious orientation of faith in the Absolute or possibly a basic attitude of mind touching on spiritual enlightenment and peace. On the other hand, the word *goga-ridatsu* (freedom from self-attachment) suggests rather the character of a practical morality. But, it is based on *gashū-ridatsu* and becomes more meaningful when it is described not as practical ethics carried out on the superficial level of human-relationships, but rather as a basic form of inner strength derived from a deep religious experience which relies on the principle of the Absolute. The next excerpt from the *Shōbōgenzō-zuimon-ki* supports this interpretation:

> The best way to give up self-attachment is to do good for the benefit of others and to act altruistically without any expectation of reward or fame. This is nothing but the basic requisite for self-detachment. To do so, we must first of all awaken to the fact that all is vanity; life is like an empty dream; time flies like an arrow; our life is transient as a dew-drop and easy to lose; time and tide wait for no man. Therefore, we should try to act in accordance with the Way, and do good to others, however insignificant it is, even for only a short span of time.

'To do good' then means giving the mind over to certain Buddhist practices, while observing the Commandments. '*Good*' in this case has a bearing on social morality. This is confirmed more positively by the next phrase 'for the benefit of others' and following it is the directive 'to act altruistically'. The nature of this altruism is discussed in more detail in the chapter, *Shishō-Bō* (*Four Provisions of Practice according to which Bosatsu urges Sentient beings to proceed toward the Buddha Way*) of the *Shōbōgenzō*. Throughout this chapter, Dōgen lays stress on the importance of practical ethics, but what should be noted is that he insists that such ethics can become effective only when firmly grounded on the principle of *muga*.

This can be read into Dōgen's conclusive assertion that such *muga* 'is nothing but the basic requisite for self-detachment.' The sentence which immediately follows this should be interpreted in conjunction with the truth of *shogyō-mujō*. The last point in the paragraph underscores the precept deduced from such a principle: 'Therefore, we should try to act in accordance with the Way, and do good to others however insignificant it is, even for only a short span of time.' As was already mentioned, questions such as: 'What are *good* and *evil*?' or 'What is a common standard for judging them?' are rejected as *keron* (idle discussion) in Buddhism. Such 'idle discussion', however, never leads directly to mere scepticism or nihilism. This fact is quite clearly recognized in the explanation of the theory of *goga-ridatsu* which is based on *muga*. In other words, setting ourselves free from self, we can acquire that basic strength with which to reject *evil* and choose *good*.

The principle of the practice of *goga-ridatsu* takes on the character of transcending *good* and *evil*. This is borne out by the truth of *kū* (emptiness) which Buddhism expounds. *Kū* is what *muga* is to be. As *muga* is the possible ground for *goga-ridatsu*, so *kū* is the theoretical ground for the transcendence of good and evil. A detailed discussion of this problem can be found in the chapter, *Shoaku-Makusa* (*Do no Evil*) of the *Shōbōgenzō*. The theory of good and evil which is developed here is so advanced that it is not easily grasped. But, the very core of this subject is that the fundamental character of the True Law of Buddha is found in *shiaku-shuzen*, and that we must through discipline, advance to the state whereby we stop doing evil without knowing it. Those who have reached such an advanced state, 'can dwell in the midst of various evils and look like men who are in bad company but cannot commit any *evil* themselves. Since refraining from *evil* actualizes a certain amount of power, evil is restrained.'

In short, it is an argument for a practical ethic which aspires to an Absolute World, while transcending the confrontation of *good* and *evil*. It never implies the annihilation of *good* and *evil*.

Rather, making a distinction between the two, it points to the world of absolute good which is not realized by following the normal standard of good and evil, only by transcending usual 'this world' definitions. In such a world, good and evil exist and yet they mean nothing; even the word *good* in the absolute good means nothing as well. In this sense, we cannot but call what is being discussed *kū* (emptiness).[1] Dōgen lays stress on the importance of this practice of *kū*, asserting that the strength with which we generate it can be traced to *goga-ridatsu*. Such a philosophical approach to moral concerns is essential to and an integral part of Dōgen's system of practical ethics.

Chapter 4

On Buddha

1 The wisdom of satori (spiritual enlightenment)

The essence of Buddhism is found in self-effacement. As we have seen so far, the physical realization of such self-effacement is found in the practice of *kū* (emptiness). To know the truth of *kū* must be our first consideration, because unless the truth of *kū* is understood, the practice of *kū* will not be realized. The reason why Buddhism is called 'the religion which pursues *satori*' can be found in this point, since *satori* is, in short, nothing but 'to know the truth of *kū*.' Our awakening to self-effacement is the essence of *satori*. On the practical level paradoxically *kū* is a necessary requisite for the attainment of *satori*. The wisdom through which one knows the truth of *kū* is called *hannya* (*Prajñā*). *Hannya* denotes wisdom, but it connotes 'the wisdom of Buddha', and 'the wisdom of *satori*'. To know the truth of *kū* is to have grasped experientially the real nature of *satori*. One who has acquired the wisdom proper to *kū* can become Buddha, and through the wisdom of Buddha, one attains *satori*. Such wisdom is called *hannya*. Then there is also the phrase 'the wisdom of *hannya*'.

Hannya is an integral concept related to the theoretical development of Buddhism, in particular Mahayana Buddhism. Approached somewhat differently, we can say quite unequivocally that the basic character of Mahayana Buddhism lies in 'the wisdom of *hannya*'. This fact clarifies the reason why Buddhism has within it such a rich, intellectual element. Needless to say, in so far as Buddhism is a religion, it is not only a matter of a rational element which depends on human intelligence, but rather it embodies an irrational element of recourse to sheer faith which is requisite to the search for salvation. Consequently, 'the wisdom of salvation' is stressed in the *Bosatsu-dō* on which the character of Mahayana Buddhism is moulded.

31

The explanation above makes us more clearly aware that the application of the rational faculties is required so that we may understand the precepts of Dōgen. Originally *Zen* Buddhism rejected the scholastic and literal interpretation of the Scriptures (*kyōten*), but, by understanding that *Zen* Buddhism demands personal effort in order to attain *satori*, we can accept it as natural that intelligence, that is, in this context, 'the wisdom of *satori*' should be an essential requisite. The image of *Monju-Bosatsu* (*Manjushiri-Bodhisattva*) is enshrined as the direct object of worship in the special exercise hall, the so-called *sōdō* of *Eihei-ji* founded by Dōgen. *Monju* is a *Bosatsu* who is very much admired as the symbolic representation of wisdom even in the secular world. The fact that this image is worshipped in the exercise hall of the *Zen* temple illustrates quite graphically how important the wisdom of *hannya* is regarded by *Zen* Buddhists. Dōgen attaches similar importance to the same concept in his precepts. This is proven by the fact that the theory of *hannya* is developed as early as the second chapter of the *Shōbōgenzō*.

The title of this chapter is *Maka-Hannya-Haramitsu*. The literal meaning of *Maka-Hannya-Haramitsu* is 'the way of the *Bodhisattva* through *kū*', and is the highest point in the theory expounded by the *Hannya* Sutra, the so-called *Hannya-kyō*. This Sutra, in turn, is the principal Sutra of Mahayana Buddhism. There are many variations of the *Hannya–kyō* but the most basic one is a work composed of 600 volumes. There is a shorter variant work of one volume, into which the essence of the entire teaching is contained in abridged form. Perhaps no other sutra has been so popular as the *Hannya-Shingyō* or merely *Shingyō*, all the more so because it is composed of only 262 Chinese characters. This second chapter of the *Shōbōgenzō* contains Dōgen's theoretical explanation of the fundamental nature of *kū* through this short sutra.

Kū as expounded in the *Hannya-Shingyō* puts emphasis on the flux of both matter and the spirit. Dōgen tells us to apply this truth to all things and to the phenomena of the world as well as to the actual affairs of everyday life. In Buddhism both matter and the spirit are represented by *go-un* (*pañca skandhāh*, the five kinds of *un*): *shiki-un, ju-un, sō-un, gyō-un, ishiki-un. Un* means classification or group, so under five headings all types of existence are classified. The material realm, including human flesh, is represented by *shiki-un*. The direct meaning of *shiki* is colour, by which we generally indicate all material existence. The other four *un* are mental components. *Ju-un* is feeling. *Sō-un* is thought. *Gyō-un* is volition. *Ishiki-un* is consciousness. There are further divisions of these five *un* into, for instance, twelve *sho* (*dvādasayatanāni*, sense fields), and eighteen *kai* (*astādasa dhātavah*, world), so that other more detailed approaches can be taken to the problem of the flux of both the body and the spirit.

Of central import is the point that what the *Shingyō* preaches is that all existence characterized by such classifications as *un, sho,* or *kai* is nothing but emptiness, that is to say, *kū*. In reverse, our body and mind, and the world around us, being composed of five *un*, twelve *sho* and eighteen *kai*, are themselves *kū*. To help us understand this fact is the basic purpose of the *Shingyō*. Dōgen, however, expresses the fear that such a quantitive method of classification evidences rigidity. So rejecting such fixed numerical conceptions, Dōgen expands the idea of emptiness on the basis of the teaching of *Dai-Hannya-kyō* (The *Great Hannya* Sutra) to include time 'past, present, future' and even the daily actions of 'walking, standing still, sitting and lying down'.

He asserts, not only that these things are empty, but, also that emptiness itself is again empty. His aim is to make the truth of *kū* permeate every physical phenomenon and the various physical actions proceeding from the human spirit. The transcendence of *kū* itself, he dares to say, is the ultimate wisdom of *hannya*. Moreover, consulting sections of *Dai-Hannya-kyō* and the verbal tradition of several Buddha formulated into *kōan*, he draws the conclusion that 'Buddha is *hannya-haramitsu* . . . the actualization of *hannya-haramitsu* is that of Buddha.' This is not Dōgen's mere dogmatic view but has its authority in the *Dai-Hannya-kyō*: '*Hannya-haramita* (or *haramitsu*) is nothing but *Butsu-Bagyabon* (*i.e.* an honorific title for Buddha). *Butsu-Bagyabon* is nothing but *hannya-haramita*.' With this as reference, it is clear that Dōgen's view is extremely significant in that he conveys what the essential Buddha character should be in Buddhism.

In what sense then, we might ask is *hannya-haramitsu* Buddha? To answer this question, we must further probe the matter of *haramitsu*. As has been previously shown, *hannya* is the wisdom of *satori* which develops through the truth of *kū*. The literal meaning of *haramitsu* is 'salvation from actual suffering'. In some cases we may be saved and in others we may save others. Therefore the meaning of *hannya-haramitsu* is that we can both be saved and save others by achieving *satori* through the experience of *kū*. Moreover it should not be forgotten that this teaching is expounded as *Bosatsu-dō*. As long as *haramitsu* is interpreted as 'to save one's own self' it is bound to be confined to the theoretical grounds of Hinayana Buddhism. It will not develop into *Bosatsu-dō* as Mahayana Buddhism until it entertains the altruistic action of saving others, because *Bosatsu-dō* is nothing else but the practice of deeds in accordance with the ideal of 'the harmony between egoism and altruism'.

Both *hannya* and *haramitsu* are direct transliterations from Sanskrit; both hold so profound an implication that it is difficult to put them into Chinese characters. Now if we dare to paraphrase their meaning as precisely as possible, this becomes 'to practise *kū* as *Bosatsu-dō*'. Therefore, Dōgen's statement that *hannya-haramitsu* is Buddha can be understood as meaning: 'an inner form expressed in practising *kū* as *Bosatsu-dō*, which is nothing but the essence of Buddha.'

As to the practice of *kū*, it is expressed most clearly in the form of *zazen*, because in *zazen*, a pure and free self is realized as standing aloof from all illusion. The definitive aim of *zazen* practice is to make us conduct even the four cardinal modes of behaviour: walking, standing still, sitting and lying down − according to the truth of *kū*. This is a difficult ideal to attain but, the practitioner of *zazen* should follow it without interruption in his daily routine, despite the inherent ups and downs of human life. Our feelings are not statically held by emotions of joy or anger. Furthermore, we are able to attain to a profound state of mind, by transforming these and other emotions, by purifying them by *kū*. Then a new way of human experience will open up to us. Thus we can bring the practice of *kū* into full play even in our daily lives and with it the wisdom of *hannya* will become activated.

But it must at the same time be acknowledged that we still cannot be released from the prison of egoism. Without the practice of altruism or at least the willingness to practise it, not only shall we not be able to step into the world of *Bosatsu-dō*, but also we will not be able to make our own world complete. This is because the misery of others will, in due course, impinge upon us; we shall not be able to improve ourselves unless we are in harmony with similar efforts of others. In this sense, we can well understand why *Bosatsu-dō* conceives of 'harmony between egoism and altruism' as an ideal for attainment. Even in altruism, without *kū* we shall not be able to live in accord with such an ideal because our keen interest in the result of our altruistic deeds is likely to have the adverse effect of egoism. We should practise altruistic deeds and yet still transcend them, in other words, should turn them into *kū* so that they may become true in themselves. Such an attitude of mind is called *jihi* (mercy) in Buddhism. Nothing is more soothing to our spirit than the *jihi* of others. The practice of *jihi* is a distinct characteristic of *Bosatsu-dō*.

To understand the truth of *kū* by means of the wisdom of *hannya* is in reality to become Buddha. But simply remaining in this state is not what Buddha should be. The truth of Buddha becomes realized through the practice of altruism by *jihi*, and this realization is to be effected first in *Bosatsu*. Buddha is believed to be the ideal form of this realization. This explains the reason why *hannya-haramitsu* is the way that the *Bosatsu* should 'be'. Thus the wisdom of *hannya* within the context of the *haramitsu* by *jihi* marks the essence of Buddha.

2 The practice of jihi (mercy)

The theory of *kū* in Buddhism has not been worked out only in relation to the wisdom of *satori*. A careful reading of the *Hannya-Shingyō* will make this fact clear. The opening section runs as follows: 'When the *Kanjizai-Bosatsu* (*Bodhisattva Avalokitesvara*) practises deep *hannya-haramita*, he discerns five *un* (*skandha*) essentially as *kū*, and releases people from all their sufferings and disasters.' The point to be considered is the phrase '(he) . . . releases people from all their sufferings and disasters.' The traditional version in wide circulation in both China and Japan translated by Genjō has this phrase, but it is maintained that the original Sanskrit version does not include it. Thus a hypothesis can be suggested that the phrase was added in translation from some reason.[1] Setting aside this problem, Dōgen must have philosophized on this Genjō version, because it was the most popular one. This reflection makes us grasp the meaning which the Sanskrit version fails to do. It is that *Kanjizai-Bosatsu*, or *Kannon*, understanding the profound truth of *kū*, performs an act of salvation through *jihi*. Thus we know that the wisdom of *satori* based upon *kū* is set forth as a premise for the act of salvation through *jihi*. This understanding on the basis of the Genjō version comes down to that of truth regarding the nature of *Bosatsu-dō*.

All *Bosatsu* are by their very nature practitioners of *jihi*, but in particular *Kannon* displays the essence of his remarkable character through such practice, so that he is called by the alternate name of *Dai-hi Bosatsu* (the *Bosatsu of Great Mercy*). In the *Hokke* or *Lotus* Sutra we are told that this *Bosatsu* is willing to transform himself in 33 ways in order to embrace all those who crave salvation. That is the reason why he has traditionally attracted so many believers. He may well be called the incarnation of *jihi*. By what practice then does *Bosatsu* bring *jihi* into full play? This is seen to be nothing but the practice of *kū*. The *Hokke* Sutra stresses this point quite emphatically. That is to say, the ground of *jihi* is derived from the wisdom of *kū*.

Jihi is a deeply felt oneness with the other by which we love him as we love ourselves, while we are equally affected by the sorrow of the other as if it were our own. In *jihi*, we empathize with the other, thereby rending the veil of separateness between us. In this sense *jihi* may be replaced with *ai* (worldy love); oneness or union is also the essential nature of *ai*. But, *ai* contains something selfish as well. By its nature, *ai* arises from attachment to the object to which it is attracted. The stronger the attachment to the object, the deeper *ai* becomes.

The fact that once *ai* fails to find its exploiting satisfaction in the object, it turns easily into its antithesis, hate, proves how self-centred *ai* is. *Jihi* is altogether different. It is absolute and can never degenerate into its antithesis, *mu-jihi* (mercilessness). It is altruistic whatever the case may be, always wishing for the happiness and welfare of the other. It is similar to *ai* in the element of oneness, but while the former has its origin in the desire to possess the other, the latter rests in the self-effacing ground of wishing good to the other. This is the reason why Buddhism rejects *ai* as lust whereas it favours *jihi* as *gangyō* (to take the oath of practice and wish the fulfilment of it) of the *Bosatsu*. The *Bosatsu* shows his essential nature in his prayer for the salvation of all those who people the world. Without this prayer, we would no longer worship him as *Bosatsu*.

Kannon-Bosatsu is the *Bosatsu* who cherishes this prayer most strongly and works the hardest for universal salvation through *jihi*. 'He . . . releases people from all their sufferings and disasters'; this single sentence in the *Hannya-Shingyō*, quite emphatically and correctly points to a prerogative. He saves all people by freeing them from the sufferings and the disasters which threaten them, and this practice of *jihi* becomes fully realized with the help of the *kū* of *hannya*. Conversely speaking, without *kū*, the full realization of *jihi* would be unattainable. Of course returning to the previous point for discussion, the importance of *ai* should be acknowledged in real matters of life. But *ai* is to be sanctified through *kū*. Such a sanctified love requires subordination to *jihi*. In this sense, *jihi* can be regarded as an ideal form of sanctified *ai*. *Kannon* is willing to answer all petitions, and desires the salvation of every human being because he actualizes such an ideal form of love.

Wisdom and *jihi*, these two qualities are of the essence of Buddha. Wisdom is the ability of the mind to understand *kū*. *Jihi* is that attitude of mind which is drawn to effecting the salvation of all people. But both are not juxtaposed as being of equal value. The wisdom of *kū* has its import only as it functions effectually to bring *jihi* to its full perfection. On the other hand, it is in *jihi* that Buddha reveals his true nature. In the *Kan-Muryōju-Sutra*, we read: 'the Buddha's mind is nothing but the great *jihi*.' *Kannon-Bosatsu* is in the process of actualizing this great *jihi*; for that great aim, he practises *kū*. Dōgen wrote the chapter, *Maka-Hannya-Haramitsu* in conformity with the above doctrine of *Shingyō*. This fact implies how strongly Dōgen urges individuals to imbibe the spirit of *Kannon* as the actualization of the *kōan*. Indeed *Kannon* must be the highest, most ideal form of the *Bosatsu-dō* that the believer could follow. By way of a concrete example pertinent to this point, in the *hattō*, the place for preaching in a *Zen* temple, *Kannon* is enshrined. The *hattō* of *Eihei-ji* is a case in point. This is not an arbitrary choice, but emphasizes the relationship between religious teaching and the essence of *Kannon*.

As we have already seen, the actualization of the *kōan* is essential to the very character of Dōgen's precepts. He preaches that such an actualization should be brought about through *kū-chi* (wisdom based on the *kū* of *hannya*). This central tenet suggests the corollary of what the ideal form of such an actualization should be. It is nothing but the practice of the true Way of the Buddha by *Kannon-Bosatsu*. The practice of *kū-chi* by *Kannon* is realized in the practice of *jihi*. To learn the essence of such practice in imitation of *Kannon* is the reason for actualizing the *kōan* of *hannya-haramitsu*. Again the practical question arising from this discussion is, in what form did *Kannon* practise the altruistic action of *jihi* and how should we go about learning it? It seems that the chapter, *Kannon* in Dōgen's work comes to grips with this problem.

There the so-called *kōan* of Ungan-Daihi is dealt with as the main focus in the discussion of the problem. The *kōan* appears in the *mondō* of Donjō Ungan, a *Zen* Master of the Tang Dynasty in China. 'For what reason does *Daihi Bosatsu* (*Kannon*) have so many hands and eyes?' *Kannon* is given various forms such as the *Jū-ichi-men Kannon*, the *Kannon who has Eleven Faces*, or the *Senju-Kannon* who has one thousand hands with an eye in every palm. Each visual representation is symbolic of the varied salvific actions carried out by *Kannon*. Here Ungan has chosen the *Jū-ichi-men Kannon* as the object of his question. Dōgen tells us that in this *kōan* we should pay attention to the phrase 'many hands and eyes'. 'Many' is many, but to Dōgen 'many' means only 'a certain number of' or 'an undecided number', because the way of *jihi* is beyond mathematical computation and the way of practising it depends upon time and circumstance.

Even if *Kannon* should have 84,000 hands and eyes, this number would still be 'a number of' to Dōgen because it is 84,000 compared with the infinite number of ways by which *jihi* can be actualized. The quantitative disparity between the numbers 1,000 and 34,000 is of no account. Both are the same, from the point of view of the given definition of Dōgen's 'a number of' as juxtaposed against infinity. Dōgen teaches that we should discover the core meaning of what Ungan meant by the word 'many' as an undecided number. A thousand hands and eyes, 11 faces, 33 different kinds of bodies of *Kannon*, these are only relative denotations in numeric form. Essentially *Kannon* can take an infinite number of forms. These innumerable forms can be interpreted as the innumerable ways of practising *jihi*. This truth is based upon the theory of *kū*, because *kū* has no limits and is indefinite.

The altruism of *kū* transcends all limitations because of its nature as *kū*. Dōgen shut himself up in the mountains, in order to write a major work to hand down to future generations. This, too, can be considered to be a great altruistic act. In *Zen* literature, there is the aphorism, 'A large thing is large, a small thing is small.' This may be paraphrased as 'everyone should conduct himself according to his ability.' As Dōgen conducted himself according to his ability, so we, persons of no importance should get along according to our ability. Dōgen emphasized that each one is able to practise *Bosatsu-dō* according to his ability, whether it be great or small. As to the actual practice of *jihi*, Dōgen expounds it in detail in *Shishō-Bō*.[2] In it Dōgen preaches that *jihi* should be shown even to flowers and birds. This is not so strange, considering his teaching that the way of *Kannon* is to be followed as an ideal. Though *Shishō-Bō* is only a single part of a more comprehensive work, its content is deceptively profound. The short *Shingyō*, a summary of the 600-volume *Hannya* Sutra, similarly carries great significance owing to its brief, though profound reference, to the practice of *jihi* in regard to the practice of *kū-chi*: namely, that 'he . . . releases people from all their sufferings and disasters.' The practice of *hannya* becomes *Bosatsu-dō*, therefore, only when it precedes and subsequently points to the practice of *jihi*.

3 Buddha and his house

Dōgen's assertion that: '*Hannya-haramitsu* is Buddha' is a life-giving principle which conveys the teaching that the wisdom of *hannya* becomes operative not merely when it is based on *kū*, but much more when it anticipates the practice of *jihi*. Indeed, nothing is more impressive about the mercy of Buddha than the teaching of the altruistic action of *jihi*. *Kannon-Bosatsu* actualizes such mercy of the Buddha. This immediately raises the question of the relationship between *Kannon* and Buddha. If '*hannya-haramitsu* is Buddha', *Kannon* must be Buddha too. Further consideration will be given to the discussion of the nature of Buddha with reference to this problem.

Buddha or *Hotoke* in Japanese is a word which originally points to Shakyamuni himself as a historical manifestation of Buddha-hood. Shakyamuni has become *Hotoke* by attaining to spiritual enlightenment. Generally speaking, a distinction is made between Shakyamuni who has attained *satori* and one who is still in the ascetical process leading to it. The latter entity is called *Bosatsu*. The etymological meaning of *Hotoke* also conveys the meaning of the enlightened nature of Buddha as 'one who has spiritual awakening' or 'one who awakened from illusion.' *Bosatsu* in contradistinction is 'one who is still devoted to studying the Way.' The point to be noted, however, is that it is man that is involved in both. Man can become Buddha. And what qualifications must a man possess? No discrimination is made here. Any man, all men will become Buddha when an earnest pursuit of the way ends in *satori*. Each man carries within himself the seeds of Buddha-hood. This is an essential point in Buddhism. The *Zen* sect is a sect grounded upon this principle and Dōgen never allowed himself to be unfaithful to it. In the chapter, *Sokushin-Zebutsu (Mind is itself Buddha)* of the *Shōbōgenzō*, Dōgen closes the discussion about the traditional idea of *sokushin-zebutsu* with the following conclusion: 'so-called Buddhas are Shakyamuni. When all the Buddhas of the past, the present and the future become Buddha, they necessarily become Shakyamuni. This means *sokushin-zebutsu*.' By way of summary it can be said that Dōgen regards all Buddhas as possessing the same character as Shakyamuni and tries to find an ideal Buddha in Shakyamuni himself. Again, turning to the traditional *Zen* temple layout for support of this premise, it is clear that generally the sanctum is situated at the centre of a *Zen* temple. Its principal image is Shakyamuni or Buddha who symbolizes the various virtues of Shakyamuni. *Eihei-ji* temple is no exception in this matter. In other words, Shakyamuni is worshipped as the consummate symbol which unites all other manifestations of Buddha.

It is equally true that all Buddhas besides Shakyamuni are worth due consideration as the object of worship. For every manifestation of Buddha should be regarded as one who has idealized or symbolized the virtues of Shakyamuni in his own particular way. In this sense, all Buddhas are Shakyamuni and this translates itself into that previously quoted statement from the *Sokushin-Zebutsu*: 'so-called Buddhas are Shakyamuni.' Dōgen never orders his followers to worship any special Buddha. He is of the opinion that to worship any Buddha, whatever Buddha he may be, necessarily leads to worship of Shakyamuni-Buddha. The Sutras of Mahayana Buddhism propound the truth of *issai-shujō-shitsu-u-busshō* (there is *'u'* the Buddha-nature *'busshō'* in all *'issai'* sentient-beings *'shujō'* entirely *'shitsu'*). Because of this, any manifestation of Buddha can be the object of worship. With such a view of Buddha, Dōgen evolves his own theory of Buddhism.

Buddhists are called to be awakened to the true nature of Buddha. Each human being by his very nature carries the Buddha-nature within, but some become awakened to it while others do not. This is the decisive difference between the two types of men. It is *Bosatsu* that makes an effort to attain to the Way of *satori*, and it is *Bosatsu-dō* that intends to construct an ideal world of Buddha-hood in co-operation with all sentient beings. Shakyamuni, following Dōgen's teaching on enlightenment, may be chosen as the foremost manifestation or representation of *Bosatsu-dō*. This is the reason why an image of Shakyamuni is set up as the object of worship in the *Zen* sect. But the distinction begs to be made that it is only one such object, not the absolute one. There are many other Buddhas who represent a symbolic realization or specific actualization of the various virtues of Buddha. It is quite natural that they should be worshipped as well. Any Buddha, so far as he is Buddha, must have realized *Bosatsu-dō* or practised it at least. In this sense, any Buddha is of equal rank with Shakyamuni. Worshipping any one of them, in turn, sets the believer on the road to Buddha-hood, which ultimately leads to Shakyamuni. It follows, therefore, that the conclusive assertion that 'Shakyamuni is *sokushin-zebutsu*' can only be grasped within the context of human effort being directed towards the Way as shown by Shakyamuni. Such effort in turn leads not merely to imitation but to the point where one has become Shakyamuni himself.

Such an approach to Buddha-hood establishes an immediate ideal as symbolized by Shakyamuni and stresses a practical phase of action represented by *Bosatsu*. A reconsideration of this relationship further implies that the truest and most ideal *Bosatsu* would reveal himself as the perfect Buddha, because such a *Bosatsu* would practise the *jihi* of Buddha through *kū*. *Kannon* is the prime example of this in Buddhism. When Buddha performs a salvific act, he must do so as *Bosatsu*. The case is the same with Shakyamuni. He is Buddha but he enters the world of human beings to journey towards *Bosatsu*. Such an understanding is widespread in Buddhism, and may well be accepted as one good answer to the dilemma man faces in contemplating the gap between ideal otherworldliness and everyday reality. Through such a conception the gap is bridged, if only a little. As *Kannon* is Buddha by his nature, he is expected to be perfect in his saving action. Dōgen has drafted the chapter on *Kannon* in the *Shōbōgenzō* from this point of view. He writes by way of exhortation, 'Don't think that *Kannon* has not yet attained to the Way. In the past world, he was the Buddha of *Shōbō-Myōbutsu* (The Buddha who clearly reveals the Truth).' With this statement as a preliminary one, Dōgen discusses in detail the countless possible acts leading to salvation.

If Buddha precedes *Bosatsu* as in the case of Shakyamuni, the fact that *Kannon* was *Shōbō-Myōbutsu* will not be strange at all. But if 'there is the Buddha-nature in all sentient beings entirely', a myriad of possible *Kannon*-like beings can be said to exist. Such a distinction warrants due consideration. In this connection, we must understand that the saying above inherently contains a basic subject for further inquiry. Dōgen deals with it in the third chapter, *Busshō (On the Buddha-Nature)* of the *Shōbōgenzō*. At this juncture in the discussion it is not imperative to go into depth. But one important point which is related to the above problem requires some comment. It is the matter of 'the house of Buddha'.

In the chapter, *Shōji (Life and Death)* in the *Shōbōgenzō*, Dōgen refers to 'the house of Buddha'; this phrase is to be understood within the context of the fundamental assertion raised in the *Busshō*, namely, the question of the Buddha-nature itself. What on earth is this 'house'? We may define it as 'the place of departure and return', that is, a place of rest. In the chapter *Shōji*, 'the house of Buddha' is referred to as an actual temple, where indeed the spirit seeks and attains calm. In our busy daily lives, it is right that we should go to a temple so that we can achieve such needed peace of mind. But, if we trace the concept further back into its origin, a more profound point can be made. The answer to this is given in the chapter, *Yuibutsu-Yobutsu (The Relation of Buddha to Buddha)* of the *Shōbōgenzō*, where Dōgen brings out the question of from where man comes and to where he returns, that is, the eternal question of the beginning and end of life. Dōgen summarizes the problem as

Born into this world, we try to solve the riddle of our existence. Why are we here? Where did life begin and where will it end? But who has the answers to such questions? Though nobody knows the actual beginning and the end of life, still he exists.

In short what Dōgen has to say is that 'no one can identify with certitude his origin or his end, and yet he is living somehow or other.' Furthermore if we draw an inference from the position presented in this chapter, it may be the following: 'We can determine neither the origin nor the end of our existence, but if this were possible, it might be *the other world*.' It might be *the other world* that we have come from and will return to. And this *other world* is nothing but 'the house of Buddha'.

We have come from 'the house of Buddha' and will return there again. If we can believe this, we will lead a full and significant life in this world. Ultimately, we cannot but believe it, because it is no use struggling to decipher the mystery of our existence. Existence remains an eternal and absolute enigma for us. In the chapter, *Shōji*, a warning is given:

> Do not try to fathom with your mind the unfathomable problem of life and death, nor explain it with words. When you throw yourself into 'the house of Buddha' casting off body and mind, giving no more thought to them, the answer due your action is offered by Buddha. You will achieve detachment from life and death by a constant following of his Way and, without effort or recourse to your mental faculties, you can become a Buddha. Once one understands this, he will no longer be attached to his narrow self.

As we have seen, the origin of the teaching on 'the house of Buddha' can be traced back to *the other world*. As no one has ever been there to ascertain the reality of that world, we can only acquiesce to the teaching of Buddha. Therefore we may regard such an unknown world as *nanimono* (something unknown). It can be argued that *nanimono* exists in that *other world*, and all sentient beings come from that *other world* carrying the attribute of *nanimono* within them. With this view in mind Dōgen expounds his theory on the Buddha-nature. In the chapter, *Busshō* quoting the phrase *issai-shujō-shitsu-u-busshō* from the Buddhist Scriptures, he explains conclusively that this is the teaching of *nanimono-ka inmo-rai*. *Inmo* translates as 'like this' or 'in such a way', and *rai* as 'has come'. So the full meaning of this phrase is that 'something unknown has come in such a way as this.' *Inmo-rai* is a *Zen* expression coined originally from a question found in the *Zen mondo* (*Zen* dialogue) 'Why have you come here?' This question, however, presupposes the affirmative judgment that, 'you have come here for some reason.'

Dōgen borrowed this term and used it as an interpretation for *shitsu-u-busshō*. Dōgen borrowed *inmo-rai* in order to provide an answer to the dilemma of: 'How can we say that there is the Buddha-nature in all sentient beings entirely?' It is because all sentient beings come from the realm of Buddha, a realm which we cannot but call *nanimono*. Because of this, there is the Buddha-nature in all sentient beings. The realm of Buddha is 'the house of Buddha'. 'House' is more familiar and concrete for us than 'realm'. In this world a temple stands for 'the house of Buddha'. As Buddhism imagines *the other world* in the light of this world, it is not strange at all that 'the house of Buddha' should exist in this world, as a place where the soul finds comfort.

Dōgen tells us that though we say we have come from *the other world*, we cannot imagine what kind of place *the other world* is in fact. This is natural in view of the truth of *kū*. *Kū* never means 'emptiness' but 'indefiniteness'. It means 'to have no limits, but to possess the possibility for becoming anything.' For this reason we are allowed to regard *the other world* as 'the house of Buddha'. Some may regard it as 'Paradise' and others as 'the Realm of God'. Both are acceptable explanations. Even if it is regarded as 'the house of Buddha', we will be able to picture it in our own way via the individual imagination. In the final analysis, it is the one *kōan* which should be actualized by each of us. In *Yuibutsu-Yobutsu*, the *kōan* which Dōgen gives us to do *kufū* on as we set about considering the beginning and the end of life is the following old saying of Buddha: 'Mountains, rivers, the earth and men have come into being in the same way. The Buddhas of the past, the present and the future, and men have been following the Way together.' In this oral teaching, there is a suggestion, to the effect, that Cosmic Nature is no more than 'the house of Buddha'. This is a logical conclusion to draw from Dōgen's thought that 'there is the Buddha-nature in all sentient beings entirely'. 'The house of Buddha' can be found everywhere in the Cosmos.

Chapter 5

Gūjin (thoroughness) and Buddha

1 Prologue

In his general remarks to the first chapter of the *Shōbōgenzō*, Dōgen introduces the problem of the *genjō-kōan*. In the second chapter he suggests that any understanding of this *genjō-kōan* should be based upon the truth of *kū*. Even the character of Buddha, he suggests, is linked to this truth. Then in the third chapter, entitled *Bosshō* (*Buddha Nature*), Dōgen carries on his exhaustive study of the true nature of the Buddha by dealing with various types of traditional *kōans*. Among them, the first two *kōans* attract our special attention. The first one is: 'There is (*u*) the Buddha-nature (*busshō*) in all sentient beings (*shujō*) entirely (*shitsu*). The Tathāgata is eternally present and unchangeable.' The second *kōan* is: 'If you wish to understand the true meaning of the Buddha-nature, you should understand the theory of the changing of time (*jisetsu innen*). If the time comes, the Buddha-nature will manifest itself.' Both *kōans* are chosen from among the most important and meaningful utterances of Shakyamuni Buddha; the former from vol. XXVII and the latter from vol. XXVIII of *Daihatsu-Nehan* Sutra (generally known as *Nehan* Sutra). Also they form a striking contrast to the twelve *kōans* which were chosen by Dōgen to follow them, all of which are those of the old Patriarchs. It is not merely the contrast between authors, but Dōgen's peculiar treatment of the first two that draws our attention. For convenience sake, we may designate them as the '*kōan* of *shitsu-u-busshō*' and the '*kōan* of *jisetsu-innen*'. A deeper analysis and inquiry into these *kōans* leads to a clearer grasp of Dōgen's originality as well as providing a bridge between Dōgen and recent philosophical study.

44

2 What is philosophy?

A definition

Let us begin with a general concept of philosophy. What is meant by the word, philosophy? What kind of learning is it? We have not yet attained to any unanimous conclusion regarding these questions. Paradoxically speaking, the diversity of definitions explains one of the characteristics of this type of learning. Philosophy is of its nature concerned with 'how to think'. Therefore each philosopher may put his own stamp on 'thinking' according to his original world view. Some may argue that such diversity in philosophy has been caused by historical circumstances and their influence. This view depends upon the fact that the Greek origins of human knowledge are well documented. Also it must be admitted that the Greeks understood all knowledge, including philosophy, to be part of a single whole. Subsequent historically documented changes point to the result of a division between philosophy and science. Further subdivisions in philosophical categories appear because of historical realities. Today, the fact that the field of science exemplifies a specialized system of minute divisions in the field of research underscores the point that such a process has developed too far. Moreover, the same tendency is likely to take place in philosophy as well. So it seems necessary for us to return to sources, in order to better deal with the issue at hand of the nature of philosophy. And for this, a definition is a prime necessity.

Love of wisdom

It depends upon each philosopher to set the starting-point of his philosophy, but, it seems most appropriate to situate it in the etymological meaning of this word and at the same time in the essence of the philosophy of Socrates. In Greek, philosophy means 'love of wisdom'. But 'love of wisdom' is essential not only to philosophy but also to every kind of genuine learning. Our desire to know the true meaning or the facts about all things; our curiosity about the nature of all the phenomena in this world provides the catalyst for learning. Such reflection, in turn, leads to the linking of the desire to know with the search for wisdom, and in unison both provide a description of the active philosopher as one who is learning the 'love of wisdom'. The problem then arises of how to distinguish philosophy from the general body of human learning. An answer to this dilemma can be found in the questing of Socrates; he is the philosopher who deals with the fundamental considerations of what should be loved and to what 'wisdom' should be directed.

To know oneself

It is said that Socrates adopted the maxim 'Know thyself' as his guiding principle during life. 'To know oneself' is a principle essential to the philosophy both of today and of the future, because philosophy is, in the final analysis, that learning which deals with the matter of oneself. If 'love of wisdom' means only 'to know the objective world as such', it is the ground of science, not that of philosophy. Some scholars may provide a definition of philosophy centring around the study of the human, but, the merely objective study of the human puts this science well within the limits of history or sociology. Others may settle for the definition of philosophy as the study of the human mind. But if the mind is dealt with only analytically, such an approach veers rather towards psychology. Philosophy is by its nature subjective, treating essentially the matter of oneself; such study being carried on by the logical mind. The logical mind is always essential. And it is the expanding of the limits of the mind which is central to philosophical activity. The fact that 'love of wisdom' is of the essence of philosophy suggests that wisdom should be required of it more than of any other type of learning. Man is apt to shrink from knowing himself, and be negligent in pursuing this objective. He is easily swayed by mood and whim. Because of this, philosophy requires constant self-awareness. This is what true 'love of wisdom' entails.

3 Yūsoku (the integration) of existence and value

Intellectualization of oneself

If the nature of philosophy is that which was described in the previous chapter, then Dōgen's precept can be studied by utilizing this same approach. Dōgen tells us that: 'To learn about the Buddha Way is to learn about oneself.' This statement is very much in accord with the earlier discussion of what philosophy expounds. 'To learn about oneself' seems to be a peculiar utterance of Dōgen. In this statement we can perceive the essence of his philosophy. 'To learn about oneself' means also 'to study oneself'. 'To learn' or 'to study' are words referring to the intellectual activity. Dōgen insists that 'to know oneself' is itself the Buddha Way. Such intellectualism lies at the centre of Buddhism. This is made clear by what is called 'the three teachings' (*san-gaku*) in Buddhism. First, *kai* teaches how to observe the commandments. Second, *jō* stresses how to acquire spiritual stability through such a way as *zazen*.

Third, *e* expounds how to understand and perceive the nature of truth by wisdom. In Buddhism, it is thought to be essential to master these three teachings. Among them *e*, which forms the nucleus of all three, is held to be the most essential; *kai* and *jō* become meaningless without *e*. *E* stresses the need for the cultivation of *chi-e* (intelligence and wisdom). The fact that *e* is put at the centre of Buddhism further underscores Buddhism's basic intellectual thrust. Both *chi* and *e* are functions related to the intellect and to its powers of recognition or perception. Buddhism holds such intellectuality within it. This is confirmed by the fact that 'becoming Buddha', the final attainment for practitioners, is another name for 'becoming the man who has been spiritually awakened or has received higher perception', in other words, 'the man who has the wisdom to understand the true way.' Historically it is clear that ideas regarding the Buddha have changed considerably through the ages. There appeared some sects which worshipped Buddha and stressed faith rather than wisdom. But true and original Buddhism is based upon intellectualism. The teaching of Dōgen aims at a return to this basic principle, and therefore may well be regarded as reactionary. Dōgen's maxim 'to learn about oneself' should be grasped with reference to this strain of intellectuality in Buddhism.

Gūjin and category

'To know oneself' is the primary requisite for the philosopher, but the implications of the phrase are limitless. In Dōgen's case, this is best expressed by the word *gūjin*, because the word and the concept definitely determine the inner quality of Dōgen's philosophy. The literal meaning of *gūjin* is 'to grasp thoroughly'. But what it implies is both very suggestive and quite profound. We come across this word frequently in the *Shōbōgenzō*. But this word was suggested to Dōgen by his master Nyojō. For example, according to an episode in *Hōkyō-ki*, Nyojō once said that the meaning of the discourses of Shakyamuni, may they be extensive or brief, is never left unperfected, and *gūjin* has been practised. But with *Nyojō, gūjin* did not develop so far as to make his philosophy creative and original while with Dōgen it played an important role in forming the central character of his philosophy. In its literal meaning, *gūjin* of itself may pass as a philosophical term but the reason Dōgen adopted it as an important idea is that it has its authority in the *Hokke* Sutra. It is found in the concrete explanation about *shohō-jissō* in the first volume of the *Hokke* Sutra.

The discourse stresses that there are ten different factors in the *jissō* of *shohō*, and that if the practitioner does not see and grasp them properly, he will not be able to attain to the true recognition of things. They are: *sō* — appearance, *shō* — nature, *tai* — substance, *riki* — ability, *sa* — activity, *in* — cause, *en* — relationship, *ka* — effect, *hō* — reward, plus *honmatsu-kukyō-tō* — the integration of all these nine factors. Moreover, the truth of this *shohō-jissō* (all things are themselves what truth should be) can be grasped only through *gūjin* (to grasp thoroughly) by the wisdom of *yuibutsu-yobutsu* (the relation of Buddha to Buddha).

What we learn from this statement are the following three things: (1) *gūjin* is an epistemological term, directed towards a way of seeing which leads to the truth about things; (2) *gūjin* needs to be practised in stages, ten of which have been categorized; (3) only the wisdom of Buddha can practise *gūjin*. Now what proves to be a key problem is the second point. Without a doubt, this second element of the inner nature of *gūjin* belongs to a sphere dealt with by the *science of category*. Category, to which we cannot easily give a precise definition, may be understood in general as the principle which determines the scope of our judgment. Using a chair, it is possible to illustrate this. Through the category of *sō*, we can draw an inference such as 'the chair is small or large': and through *shō*, it can be ascertained whether 'the chair is stable or unstable.' *Tai* allows for a judgment regarding use, 'it is a chair for children', while *riki* assesses strength, 'the chair is strongly built.' *Sa* relates to action, 'it has a good pivoting device or it can be raised or lowered', while *in* considers causality, 'why the chair is put here', for example, at the request of a child. *En* moves into the realm of relationships which affected the existence of the chair, perhaps some advice from a friend. *Ka* probes the realm of effect and the 'result of the interaction between the cause and circumstance', for example, the choice of a good chair. *Hō* takes off into the less concrete realm of attainment or 'reward by endeavour', the user's advancement in scholarly pursuits. At this point, after moving through categories one through nine, it is necessary to pause before dealing with the final category, *honmatsu-kukyō-tō*.

Yūsoku (integration)

The tenth category, *honmatsu-kukyō-tō* means in its literal sense that all the categories from the first through the ninth are, in the final analysis, equal. Equality in this case means that all these nine categories are integrated into one entity. Certain Buddhist phrases express this idea quite well: 'all is one' (*issai-sokuitsu*), 'one is all' (*issoku-issai*), and 'all is integrated into one whole' (*yūsoku-ichinyo*). *Honmatsu-kukyō-tō* should be dealt with in this context as embodying a central Buddhist tenet of integration. The nine categories just delineated moreover are essentially the same as those traditionally found in Western philosophy. Only the tenth category, that of *honmatsu-kukyō-tō* is in striking contrast to the preceding nine. In what sense is it so different? It is in the sense that the tenth category is synthetic while the preceding ones are all analytical. Generally speaking, the approach to knowledge in the West can be said to be analytical. To be sure, this has encouraged scientific progress, but at the same time it has prevented Occidentals from perceiving the excellence of intuition. The approach to learning in the Orient has not always disregarded the importance of analysis, but, as a whole, its distinguishing characteristic is that of understanding through synthesis. This holds true in the instance of the problem of category with which we are dealing now. Buddhists set down categories, as we saw above, but by integrating them into a single whole, namely, through *yūsoku-ichinyo* (integration into one), they try to grasp truth as one. Such knowledge as described in *Hokke* Sutra is called *nyojitsu-chiken* (to see and know realities as they are).

Jissō of gūjin

As long as we depend upon the approach of synthetic judgment through *yūsoku* (integration), the number of categories means nothing. It better accords with the true meaning of *honmatsu-kukyō-tō* to judge the single entity in relation to the whole, taking circumstances and occasions into consideration. Dōgen put special emphasis upon this point. He speculated, and drew inferences always along this line. The chapter, *Shohō-Jissō*, in the *Shōbōgenzō* provides some clarification on this matter in describing an impressive scene Dōgen came across in China. Dōgen deals with the theory of ten kinds of *categories* as a thematic *kōan* and discusses it as follows: 'Originally, *honmatsu-kukyō-tō* is another name for *shohō-jissō*. All things should be learned in *yūsoku-ichinyo*, because to learn Buddhism means nothing but to learn *yūsoku*. In short, Dōgen asserts that *shohō-jissō*, the fundamental tenet of Mahayanist Buddhism, should be understood within the context of the nature of *honmatsu-kukyō-tō*. According to the original statement found in the *Hokke* Sutra, the '*Jissō*' of *shohō* is to be grasped through ten kinds of *categories*.' Dōgen, however, develops this differently, insisting that only the last category should be accorded respect. This is reasonable enough, because the gist of the original statement from the *Hokke* Sutra is that we can attain to true knowledge (*nyojitsu-chiken*) through the practice of the *gūjin* of the ten *categories*, therefore *honmatsu-kukyō-tō* is the main factor in the pursuit of true knowledge. Adhering to this position makes the analytical categories less significant and nullifies their absolute character. In fact, the Sutra seems to arrange the number of categories in a system of nine built on the principles of analysis, plus one which approaches integration through synthesis. Dōgen accepts these analytical categories, but he would never be restricted by them. He insists that we can attain to the truth only through a final synthesis of the whole. This presupposes the integration of diverse properties with their different relationships to time and circumstance. He proclaims that this, that is to say, *yūsoku*, is fundamental to *gūjin* and the *jissō* of *shohō* is attained through it. In the chapter of *Shohō-Jissō* of the *Shōbōgenzō*, beginning with the statement that what the Patriarchs preached is the *jissō* of *gūjin*, Dōgen develops a detailed discourse on the truth of *shōhō-jissō* under the heading of the principle of *yūsoku*.

Yūsoku of existence and value

The character of *gūjin* in Dōgen's teaching is that of seeing and knowing the *jissō* of *shohō* through *yūsoku*. The *jissō* of *shohō* is a phrase derived from the Chinese '*shohō-jissō*'. The latter means, as we saw in section 3, chapter 2 and section 3, chapter 3 in this work, that *shohō* is *jissō*; all things (*shohō*) are themselves what truth should be (*jissō*). This *jissō* could be grasped as it is, only by an in-depth study of *shohō* in the principle of *yūsoku-ichinyo*. Then *shohō-jissō* can be seen as not inconsistent with Dōgen's *jissō* of *shohō*. Indeed in one chapter of the *Shōbōgenzō*, under the heading, *Shohō-Jissō*, Dōgen slowly brings his own views of the *jissō* of *shohō* to light through the explanation as to how *shohō* is *jissō*.

When we say '*shohō* is *jissō*', however, we may well wonder whether the distinction between existence and value may disappear. If any mode of existence (*shohō*) is accepted as it is (*jissō*) and all the gradations of value, for example, good and evil, beauty and ugliness are *jissō*, value judgments about morality would not be required. Neither art, based upon the values of beauty and ugliness, nor science which winnows the false from the true, would depend upon value judgments. Art and science would therefore lose their justification for existence. Any inclination, moreover, to disregard ethical values would lead to chaos in the social order and therefore, to the destruction of the human world itself. Buddhism does not disregard the gradation of value. It expects us to move into the higher world of value judgments through the integration of existence and values. Accepting the gradations of values as they are, but, not rendering them static, Buddhism hopes we may find our way into the world of the absolute value of the Buddha. Actually, the values of the real world cannot escape being relative in the sense that they are in touch with existence. For example, the values of good and evil acquire their meaning in relation to existence; even honesty, that distinction between truth and falsehood, may lose its more obvious meaning in the case of a doctor who examines a terminally ill patient.

Value judgments concerning beauty and ugliness may vary according to the aesthetic feeling of the respective viewers. This is the reason why the critics of various schools make such divergent comments. The perception of truth or falsehood and the judgment which follows may depend upon a certain premise, that of two contradictory pieces of truth accepted often as true at one and the same time. What is called here 'the aesthetic feeling of the respective viewers' or 'a certain premise' are, in short, elements concerned with existence outside of the realm of pure value, in the sense that the person who feels *is*, or the premise *exists*. Therefore we know that in general, actual value can have significance only in relation to existence. If so, the truth of things, namely, the *jissō* of *shohō* can only be grasped through some process of synthesis.

This holds true in the realm of general knowledge. For example, our knowledge of water, that its constituents are hydrogen and oxygen or that it attains its maximum density at four degrees centigrade, pertains to scientific value, having nothing to do with water's artistic or practical value. What a painter takes an interest in are the shades in the colour of the water in the scene he is going to draw. For the *sakē* brewer, the matter of primary concern is whether the water is suitable for the brewing process. In short, even our knowledge of water works only in relation to certain relative values. It is well to note at this point that dealing with pure knowledge leads us only to abstract and idle discussion. Therefore, if we are going to see and grasp existence as it is, we should do so through *yūsoku-ichinyo* and not by separating existence from value. In this way, if value is grasped, and integrated with existence, all existence will be seen to be relative, because as the mode of existence changes, its value also changes and vice versa. In the light of such relativity, gradations of existence will disappear and be equalized. '*Shohō* is *jissō*' is a theory based upon such an approach to existence. When the actual world is seen in comparison to the absolute world, which should be regarded as that of Buddha, it follows that all existence is equal and that because of this equality, any form of existence can be accepted into the absolute world of Buddha.

The meaning of equality

Shohō-jissō rooted in the principle of equality may be accepted as natural in view of the Buddhist religious ideal, because it has its theoretical ground in *jihi* and salvation for all humankind. *Jihi* is, as we saw in the previous chapter, often confused with *ai*. But *jihi* is absolute, because it originates in the Buddha mind while *ai* is relative due to its egoistic nature, which finds expression in lust. This absoluteness of *jihi* comes from its transcendence of the gradations relative to values. The earnest desire to bestow salvation upon everyone, however unworthy, is of the true nature of the *jihi* of Buddha. The way of salvation is open to all. Transcendence by *shohō-jissō* derives from its pursuit of the lofty idea of religion, not from its disregard for actual values. This fact should be clear from the explanation developed so far. If the fact is misunderstood the result is a blind equality. Even baseness will be sanctioned and public morals thrown into confusion.

Dōgen cautions us severely against such an erroneous attitude. It is told that he dared to expel those followers who had chosen such a mistaken course. Gradation in dealing with values is necessary when coping with the real world. The essence of *shohō-jissō* rests in that it admits that actual values together with their gradations lead to salvation. In the case of a wicked man, if he repents of his sin and directs his steps toward good, we can say that his sin itself is the cause of his being set on the way towards Buddha. It may sound paradoxical, but, we dare to say that the more sinful one is, the more virtuous one will be able to become. If one boasts of his own virtue and becomes arrogant, one may be led astray forever. Although the so-called good and evil in this world cannot but be relative, nevertheless a definite distinction between good and evil, beauty and ugliness needs to be established so as to clarify the nature of integration as developed in Dōgen's philosophy.

The practice of the absolute good

Buddhism preaches a way toward absolute value, as the way toward Buddha. Concretely the *Shichi-butsu-tsūkaige* contains the answers to certain questions about this from a practical point of view. The teaching that we should not do evil deeds, but good ones is clearly stated. Possibly because of this initial perception it is apt to be viewed as merely a treatise on moral philosophy. It is vastly different, however, for Buddhism, which embodies a moral philosophy, aspires higher to the world of absolute value. Conversely, in such a system moral value rediscovers its own true value when it is set against absolute value, for the practice of these true values is nothing but the way of Buddha. 'We should not do evil deeds, but good ones.' This maxim, to be sure, contains a certain overt similarity to a tenet from moral philosophy or mere moral activism. Nevertheless this apparent similarity stops when the practice of the good is realized, and illuminated by the absolute world. Dōgen makes an in-depth study about this and constructs his probing into a highly formulated theory in the chapter, *Shoaku-Makusa (Do no evil)* of the *Shōbōgenzō*.

4 Yūsoku (the integration) of existence, becoming and practice

Gūjin in Dōgen's philosophy is an important key to the understanding of his theory regarding *busshō* (Buddha-nature). Of the two *kōans* mentioned in section 1 of this chapter, that of *shitsu-u-busshō* will be dealt with first. Once again the same sections of the *kōan* will be quoted in their entirety:

> There is (*u*) the Buddha-nature (*busshō*) in all sentient beings (*shujō*) entirely (*shitsu*). The Tathāgata is eternally present and unchangeable.

In the first section of the chapter, *Busshō* of the *Shōbōgenzō*, Dōgen treats this as the first principle of a thematic *kōan* and develops his personal theory regarding the Buddha-nature. At the beginning he explains the ultimate purport of this *kōan* using the Patriarchs' word *in-morai*, which means that something unknown has come in such a way as this, a concept which has already been discussed in section 3, chapter 4 of this work. Continuing this, he swells upon the meaning of *shujō* (all existence) and *busshō*, and the relation that exists between them. He begins with the explanation of the terms *shujō* and *shitsu-u* with reference to the accepted distinctions of *ujō* (things having feeling), *gun-u* (all things), *gun-rui* (living things) and *gun-jō* (animate things). Then he discusses how he coined the term *shitsu-u* from the Chinese characters which mean 'is (*u*) . . . entirely (*shitsu*)', or 'all existence'. Finally he draws the conclusion that '*shitsu-u* is *busshō* and one aspect of *shitsu-u* is designated as *shujō*.'

In the discourse of Dōgen so far, the following three points attract special attention. The first is that 'one aspect of *shitsu-u* is designated as *shujō*.' If one aspect indicates *shujō* as 'living things', there may well be another aspect which exists around these things and supports them. Indeed Dōgen does not forget to refer to this just before the conclusion of the discussion: 'The term *shitsu-u* can be substituted for the terms *shujō* and *gun-u*.' *Gun-u* indicates things of this other aspect. In short, both *shujō* and *gun-u* occupy all parts of *shitsu-u*. This idea is founded on the orthodoxy of Buddhism. In Buddhism, *shujō* means a living thing which has rebirth through the transmigration of the soul and *gun-u* stands for a circumstantial form of existence which allows for survival 'as is', but not transmigration. Therefore Dōgen's idea is completely in accord with Buddhist theory, and his teaching that 'one aspect of *shitsu-u* is designated as *shujō*' may also be accepted as quite natural.

The second point to be concerned with is that '*shitsu-u* is *busshō*.' There are two problems to be considered regarding this point. In the original thematic *kōan*, the relationship between *shujō* and *busshō* is designated as one of inclusion; there is *busshō* in all *shujō*; whereas, here the term *shujō* seems to be replaced by *shitsu-u* without any apparent reason. But this may be permissible, because if *shitsu-u* as a higher concept means 'all existence' including *gun-u*, the scope of *shujō* will be superseded by this broader version of *shitsu-u*. This in turn better accords with the understanding of *gūjin* which Dōgen tries to apply to every problem. There may, however, arise another question, namely, that of whether this formulation leads to a contradiction, if it is accepted. We are necessarily led to concur from this theory that there is *busshō* in other forms of existence besides *shujō*, such as *gun-u* in *shitsu-u*. Despite the appearance of contradiction, Buddhism does not consider it as a contradiction but as an acceptable given. This is suggested by the following Buddhist text that 'all the grasses, trees, and countries can become Buddha.' This approach is typical of Buddhism. It is with such a traditionally Buddhist approach to a matter as a basis for thought that Dōgen explores the subject.

The third point to consider involves another aspect arising from the same point. In the statement '*shitsu-u* is *busshō*', the original term *shujō* can be replaced by *shitsu-u*, as we have seen, but may not this substitution suggest a difference in the essential meaning of the thematic *kōan*, 'there is *busshō* in *shujō*'? To repeat, '*shitsu-u* is *busshō*' parallels in its meaning '*shutō* is *busshō*' so far as *shujō* is *shitsu-u* is concerned, but another problem remains to be solved. 'There is' in the *kōan* cannot be equal to 'it is' in Dōgen's formulation, or can it? The basis for such a change may also be called into account. Such a question emerges as a fundamental problem requiring consideration. One answer is that Dōgen was afraid that '*there is*' would not express with precision what the Sutra has to say.

We can interpret the Chinese sentence of the Sutra concerned in two ways. One is 'there is *busshō* in all *shujō* entirely' and the other is 'all *shujō* has *busshō* entirely.'

'There is' explains the locus of existence as residing in the subject, *busshō*, and requires an adverbial phrase 'in *shujō*' to complete its meaning. On the other hand, '*shujō* has *busshō*' means '*shujō* includes *busshō* in itself.' Both expressions show, after all, a separate mode of existence inherent in the relationship between *busshō* and *shujō*. *Busshō* and *shujō* are then understood as designating separate modes of existence implying two different natures.

Despite such hypothesizing, neither interpretation, however, is in accord with the true import of the Sutra. Chinese of the Sutra never talks about such separate modes of existence as 'there is *busshō*, namely, as a foreign substance, in *shujō*' or as '*shujō* has *busshō*, namely, a foreign substance, in itself.' The *Daihatsu-Nehan* Sutra on which the authority of this thematic *kōan* rests clarifies this fact; it says, 'If we say there is *busshō* in *shujō*, each as a separate thing, the truth cannot be grasped at all. Why? Because *shujō* is *busshō* and *busshō* is *shujō*' (vol. 35). In short, even if we say 'there is *busshō*' or '*shujō* has', it is merely a matter of verbalization. As expressing a mode of true existence, *busshō* is *shujō* and *shujō* is *busshō*. They never designate separate existences. On the authority of the inner meaning of the Sutra, Dōgen draws the conclusion that '*shitsu-u* is *busshō*' and from this formulation he implies that '*shujō* is *busshō*.'

Throughout his detailed discussion of the Buddha-nature, Dōgen tries to make clear the integration of *shujō* and Buddha. He deals with this problem of integration through a consideration of the way of existence based on the true meaning of the Sutra. And yet despite such argument, the reason why the relation between *shujō* and *busshō* should be altered from 'there is' to 'it is' has not been completely clarified, other than by the fact of appealing to the authority of the Sutra. '*There is*' expresses the very fact of existence while '*it is*' expresses the relationship between things which exist. The latter expression generally consists of terms denoting a substance and its attribute. The theory that '*shujō* is *busshō*' is justified as a formal judgment when we regard *shujō* as substance and *busshō* as its attribute. But, this theory cannot be justified except as a preliminary one which assumes that the relatedness of Buddha and *shujō* is identical. In fact preliminary assent is given to this position in Buddhism. That is why one can affirm that '*shujō* becomes Buddha.'

The process by which this is accomplished is *jōbutsu*. Important to note is the fact that Buddhism can never be grasped so long as we adhere to the Western viewpoint that God and man are completely different in their natures. Buddhism rejects this notion and instead stresses that one can become Buddha. At this point in the discussion, the theory of becoming must be given consideration. The problem is inherent in the way of *becoming*, or 'how to become'. Generally speaking, what we call existence can *be* only through *becoming*. Existence 'has become' and 'will become'. Existence *is* in *time*. Dōgen calls this *uji* (being-time): *u* means 'exist' and *ji* 'time'. The chapter on *uji*, in the *Shōbōgenzō* develops the theory of the relationship between existence and time, beginning with the famous sentence, 'Time is existence; existence is time.' Every existence therefore *is* in process in time and the process of time *is* 'known' by how it *exists*. The ramifications of Dōgen's *uji* should be understood theoretically as providing a basis for the subjective attainment of actual knowledge about a 'thing'. Dōgen's assertion that true knowledge can be attained in *gūjin* through *yūsoku* can be grasped more clearly, when viewed in connection with the theory of *uji*.

Pushing the argument further, Dōgen's teaching is even applicable to general knowledge. The expression about existence, *'there is'*, is a judgment accompanied by the question 'where', but we should not fail to see it as also accompanied by another question 'when', one related to time. *'There is'* is a judgment which can be fulfilled by answers to 'when' and even 'where' in the present as well as in the past and the future. We can never deal with existence without discovering the deep involvement with time. There is no existence without some causal relationship. Here is found the reason why Dōgen insists that we practise *gūjin* while considering ten categories which address the dual questions of perceiving matter and grasping what it means to exist.

In that knowledge as well regarding the empirical world of experience, the knowledge of existence is necessarily attended by time. In the knowledge of ideas, however, the case is quite different. 'Time' is not involved and 'space' dissolves into the world of ubiquity. Nothing is regulated by limiting concepts such as 'when' or 'where'. Fantastic thoughts may have free rein because of this. An entire world can be imagined if such restraints are lifted. It would be an ideal world in which nothing would exist but Buddha and the Buddha-land. The former would be the highest and purest ideal of a world to be attained by we, human beings, and the latter would be an ideal world which always had eternity and absoluteness in view. Both are worlds where limitations such as 'when' or 'where' are meaningless. This ideal world would be completed by 'whenever' and 'wherever', that is to say, by timelessness and ubiquitousness.

In the *Hokke* Sutra such a fantastic world is described, one far beyond the real limitations of time and space, a world in which the various Buddhas are also universal proponents of eternal life. This should not be regarded as the same as an idle fantasy in which one indulges in self-complacency. Such aspirations towards a world and an existence without limits are based upon the universal belief by humankind in an eternal existence. When such human longings touch reality, mere fantasy is disdained. If not, the pursuit of fantasy would obliterate the real fabric of life. The reason why the *Nehan* Sutra preaches that *'shujō* is *busshō* and *busshō* is *shujō'* can be understood in the light of his argument. Not only *shujō* but all existence must be *busshō* in view of the theory that 'all the grasses, trees, and countries can become Buddha.' The true meaning of Dōgen's saying that *'shitsu-u* is *busshō'* is further illuminated by considering this connection.

Here we must remember anew that the first principle of the thematic *kōan* in the chapter on *Busshō* consists of two propositions: (1) There is (*u*) the Buddha-nature (*busshō*) in all sentient beings (*shujō*) entirely (*shitsu*); (2) The *Tathāgata* is eternally present and unchangeable. The latter proposition indicates the nature of the existence of Buddha as transcending the limitations of time and space. By this proposition, the ubiquitous existence of *busshō* is clarified for us. *Busshō* exists 'whenever' and 'wherever'; if not, the relative meaning which the latter proposition has for the former one will not become clear. These two propositions support and clarify one another. This basic theory is nothing but a restatement of *soku-itsu* (all is one) as found in the *Nehan* Sutra. Through *soku-itsu* we can arrive at the profound realization that there is *busshō* in *shujō*, because *shujō* is *busshō*. The truth of this is shown more clearly upon examination of the second principle of the thematic *kōan* which states:

> If you wish to understand the true meaning of the Buddha-nature, you should understand the theory of the changing of time (*jisetsu-innen*). If the time comes, the Buddha-nature will manifest itself.

Dōgen presents his own interpretation of this *kōan* and develops it as part of his own teaching. The most characteristic point we should take notice of is that Dōgen interprets 'if the time comes' as 'the time has already come.' The equivalent in Chinese for 'if the time comes' is *nya-kushi*, and for 'the time has already come' the term is *kishi*. Dōgen states that: 'we may safely use *kishi* for *nyakushi*.' One problem, again semantic, needs to be addressed, for if we literally interpret the original section of the *kōan*, then *nyakushi* must be 'if ...comes', not 'has already come'. This is to be viewed as consistent with the theory of *soku-itsu* in the *Nehan* Sutra. There, after preaching that *shujō* is *busshō* and *busshō* is *shujō*, the Sutra comments on this problem as follows: 'the difference between *purity* (*busshō*) and *impurity* (*shujō*) depends upon the difference of time. When our soul and body are *impure*, we are *shujō* and when they are pure, we are Buddha.' According to this section in the original text, the difference between *shujō* and *busshō* is attributed to a difference in time; no reason for interpreting *nyakushi* as *kishi* can be found here. Then on what basis can Dōgen's interpretation be built? Is it merely a game, a substitution of words?

By way of an approach to an answer, we should understand this problem by bearing in mind the distinction between actual knowledge and knowledge which is idealized. To be sure, in the realm of empirical knowledge, *nyakushi* cannot be *kishi*. Time is a necessary factor, a limitation to the understanding of actual existence. All 'becoming' is in the stream of time; even mutation has its own chance only in time. But, in the realm of ideal knowledge, existence which transcends the real, especially when it is knowledge of the divine world, can be arrived at regardless of time. We can become Buddha, to be sure, but it is not through such a time encrusted process as that found in the world of matter, nor through the fulfillment of certain requirements as in artistic creation, but through our awakening to the Buddha-nature, that is to say, the realization of the nature of Buddha himself. Therefore the awareness of the Buddha-nature which leads to its attainment cannot but be the result of self-awakening, quite unlike an awareness of existence which we know in actual time.

Through a spiritual awakening, *it* becomes *itself*, that is to say, *busshō* becomes *busshō* itself. This awakening must be understood to depend upon the transcendence of time, because such awakening is in its essence beyond time. Moreover, it must involve experiencing a mode of existence which has the nature of *kishi*, that is to say, existence which is in the state of 'whenever' or 'wherever'. Viewed in relationship to the process of awakening, this state of existence is designated as *nyakushi*; in its original state beyond time, it becomes *kishi*. To put it in another way, *busshō* depends for its realization on the subject's awakening to it; this state of existence is designated as *nyakushi*. But in the context of the statement that *shujō* is *busshō* in its essence, the time when *busshō* presents itself is always now. Therefore this state of existence is always *kishi*. If not, *busshō* cannot provide the answer to the universality of the call to awakening for all persons. If the statement in the *Nehan* Sutra 'if the time comes' suggests the possibility of the true appearance of *busshō*, this time has in actuality already come. The chance of attaining to it is always *now*. It only depends upon our awakening to it. This is what Dōgen intends to say by substituting *kishi* for *nyakushi*.

As we have seen, *time* is always present now, always *kishi*. Then what concretely is it that such an understanding of time suggests? This is a problem which requires further study. Time in the original statement means literally 'the time when *busshō* presents itself.' But in what way will *busshō* actually present itself? The crux of the problem is that of recognition. As *'sitsu-u* is *busshō'*, the appearance of *busshō* must be in *sitsu-u*, and in this case, *shujō* in *sitsu-u*. To express it more specifically, 'we ourselves' or the subjective element requires careful consideration. It is essential for *busshō* to appear in us. Dōgen has this to say in one of his sermons as we saw in section 3, chapter 5 in this work: 'To learn about the Buddha Way is to learn about oneself.'

The fundamental aim of Buddhism is that of leading us through the process of self actualization. This means that we, ourselves, become Buddha. Buddhism always holds out such an expectation for humankind. What the actual manifestation of *busshō* means will be found in the fact of becoming Buddha. The moment of this manifestation is without a doubt that moment when we attain to the Buddha-nature. Taking this moment into consideration, Dōgen interprets 'if the time comes' (*nya-kushi*) as 'the time has already come' (*kishi*), with full assurance that 'there can be no doubt about it.' The tone of this strong assertion is enough to inspire the seeker to believe that he is able to become Buddha at any moment. 'At any moment', this posits the actual transcendence of time, which is what is also meant by the statement: 'the time has already come.' Such an interpretation can only be possible in relationship to the theory of *yūsoku*, that is, the integration of two realizations (*genjō*). The first realization is that we, ourselves, become Buddha and the second is that the Buddha is present as itself in us. The *Nehan* Sutra further states that: 'If you wish to understand the true meaning of the Buddha-nature, you should understand the theory of the changing of time (*jisetsu-innen*).' If we interpret the changing of time, in this case, to be the moment when we ourselves realize Buddha-nature by ourselves, the true implication of this statement will be better understood.

Dōgen explains *innen* in terms of *shitsu-u*. This is reasonable; we do actualize *busshō* in ourselves through the medium of *shitsu-u*, that is, *shitsu-u* working as *innen*. As was discussed in section 3, chapter 2, Reiun-Shigon, the Zen Master, grasped 'the Way' at the sight of some peach blossoms in full bloom and Kyōgen-Shikan, another Zen Master, attained spiritual enlightenment when he heard a small stone hit a bamboo tree. In other words, they felt and 'grasped' *busshō* in seeing the peach blossoms and hearing the sound of a stone striking a bamboo tree. *Busshō* actualizes itself everywhere and in everything in this world.

It is only when *shitsu-u* is *busshō* that we are able to actualize *busshō* in ourselves. 'If the time comes, the Buddha-nature will manifest itself.' This statement finds its reason in the fact that 'the time has already come', that is to say, 'the time is now.' Only by actualizing this time of *now* will the 'Buddha-nature manifest itself.' This manifestation is, therefore, deeply inherent in the theory of *genjō* (actualization).

Even if *shitsu-u* is *busshō*, it will never manifest itself as *busshō* unless we actualize *busshō* by ourselves. Through our *doing* or practice of the Buddha Way, *busshō* becomes realized. *Busshō* becomes realized because *shitsu-u is* originally *busshō.* If *shitsu-u* is *busshō*, the time when *shitsu-u* becomes realized is always *now*. Time is *now* forever. This idea is essential to the content of *shushō-ittō* which Dōgen advocates. *Shōka* (Buddha) is not in the future. Of course Buddha cannot be in the past. While *becoming*, one practises the Way in the present moment. 'Is' is accompanied by 'become' and 'become' is based upon 'doing'. A failure to see and grasp this trilogy as one, makes the attainment of true knowledge impossible.[1]

Chapter 6

Racial ground

1 Gūjin and yūgen (profundity)

Gūjin is not only at the centre of Dōgen's thought, but also a remarkable feature of it. As we have seen, Dōgen tries to make a full and thorough study of a problem so as to attain to the ultimate truth of enlightenment. This profound, far-reaching pursuit of truth by Dōgen also results in denying his students the use of a simple approach to understanding his preaching. The *Shōbōgenzō* is universally held to be one of the most difficult works ever written in Japan. This comes partly from its profundity (the *gūjin* nature of it) and partly from the terse, suggestive mode of expression Dōgen adopts in it. One question raised by these considerations is whether or not Dōgen consciously chose to be difficult. It does look as if the monumental study was the product of his peculiar talent and character, but, we should note that it developed from a distinct tradition.

Buddhism encouraged those who took it seriously to delve into areas which were vague, often impenetrable, and this in turn resulted in a vagueness of language and expression. In Buddhism, the concepts of *mu* or *kū*, and the depth of speculation about the problem of death inevitably lead into a world which is neither simple nor easily accessible to ordinary language. The Buddhist sutra epitomizes the theory of *gūjin*. A point to be noted is that in contrast to Chinese Buddhism where numberless references to *gūjin* are found in sutras, Japan developed the same core concept in its own peculiar way. Why did this happen? Any answer would have to develop from a consideration of the different racial characteristics of the Chinese and Japanese.

The profound nature of Dōgen's thought finds its ground in a certain characteristic which can be found deep within the psyche of the Japanese.

61

It is best expressed by *yūgen*, a term peculiar to *Nōh*, which implies a quiet, elegant and profound beauty. These attributes are equally those which describe *gūjin*. To approach the subject in another way, both *yūgen* and *gūjin* are derived from the unique racial character of the Japanese. In one of the songs or *yōkyoku* of the *Nōh* play *Hōkazō* (*Hōka Priest*), there is a passage which contains a reference to the *Zen kōan*: 'Within, to grasp the truth in the depth of *yūgen*. Without, to enjoy the quietude of *zazen*.' This fragment of the song indicates that for the author of the *Nōh* play the nature of *kōan* and the quality of *yūgen* are the same. If so, all of Dōgen's precepts in the *Shōbōgenzō* must be identifiable with *yūgen*, according to the position that all 90 chapters of the work are nothing but sections of a single book of *kōan*.

Yūgen is peculiar to *Nōh* and its songs, *yōkyoku*, and yet the *Nōh* qualities of stillness and beauty find the ground of their being in the very source of the *gūjin* of Dōgen. One of the reasons why Dōgen's *gūjin* has something in common with the *yūgen* of *Nōh* may be attributed to the spiritual climate of the age, that of the Kamakura era (1192-1333). The Kamakura era, during which Dōgen lived and died, was more influenced by Buddhism than any other period in Japan's history. This age, moreover, saw Japan not only adhering rigorously to Buddhism, but also moulding it to Japan's unique culture. Many religious sects well adapted to the Japanese temperament were established at this time, all of them being free from slavish imitation of Chinese Buddhism. Though varied in their doctrinal context, they were similar in that they adapted themselves to Japanese religiosity. Among them, Dōgen's religious thought towered above all the rest because of its deep philosophical speculation geared to adapting Buddhism to Japanese needs.

The same tendency can be perceived in the world of literature. The literature of the Kamakura era teems with the doctrine and tenets of Buddhism. *Nōh* is the best example of a highly refined art form drawing on the profound depths of Buddhism, and this pursuit in turn resulted in the formulation of the artistic concept, *yūgen*. The *Nōh* play and its *yōkyoku* chants reached a definitive form shortly after the Kamakura era. Actually it was in the Muromachi era (1336-1573) which followed that Buddhism in the form of *Zen* spread its influence into such art forms as the tea ceremony (*chano-yu*), landscape gardening and architecture. In the turbulent period after the Muromachi era, people began to take a realistic view of the world which developed during the Edo era (1603-1867) into an attraction for Confucian thought.

Such a historical overview of Japanese religious thought strongly indicates a linear progression. Consequently a question may be raised as to whether *gūjin* and *yūgen*, if they are deeply involved with the *Zeitgeist*, have any actual significance for us today? The answer should be in the affirmative, but, with a reservation, that is to say, that as a norm they seem to be retaining their value today. If so, the degree to which an Occidental can appreciate them fully can be brought into question. Setting aside the problem of *gūjin* for the moment, *yūgen* as found in *Nōh* is peculiar to Japan. Even among the Japanese, there are not many who can appreciate *Nōh* and its linguistically complicated songs. The indifference of some Japanese to them, however, doesn't mean that they are meaningless. Indifference can be attributed to two causes: first, the traditional arts require a highly developed artistic sense for appreciation, and second, the traditional means for developing such an artistic sense is missing in contemporary Japan. The obstacles confronting the non-Japanese student of Japanese art or culture are fundamentally different. The primary obstacle is the totally different quality of sensibility. This does not infer that understanding Japanese culture is impossible for the non-Japanese. The point to remember is that dissimilarities in culture, temperament or sensibility, once recognized as such, call forth a greater effort on the part of individuals who confront another culture. In this sense, no matter how difficult it may be, it is essential for Occidentals who want to grasp the specific racial character of the Japanese, to direct their attention to the complexities of *Nōh*.

There are also some Occidental scholars who hold a similar opinion. An apt example is Dr W. Scott Morton, professor Emeritus of Seton Hall University. In the chapter 'Theatre' of his book, *The Japanese – How they Live and Work* (Charles E. Tuttle, Tokyo, 1974), he states: 'The theatre in Japan probably offers a wider variety of living forms, from classical *Nō* to night-club, than can be found anywhere else in the world.' He emphasizes the importance of *Nōh* in connection with the problem under discussion and continues, 'Everyone should see a *Nō* play at least once', in order to understand the Japanese. Comparing *Nōh* with classical Greek Tragedy, he draws the following conclusion: 'The Greeks appeal to reason, even though the chorus dance out their emotions; the Japanese appeal to intuition, even though the actors use words.' 'Greek tragedy relies on the clear verbal exposition of motive and character' so that we can approach the drama with logical reasoning and understanding. On the other hand, we must approach *Nōh* with intuition, because it 'uses mime, stylised dance and chanting to suggest by subtle and indirect means the mood of the piece.'

In fact, *Nōh* aims at expressing the greatest truths through amazing economy of means. It requires us to grasp with intuition the profound meaning of the whole context of the drama. This special character of *Nōh* survives even today in the daily feelings and behaviour of the Japanese. Though they have become remarkably westernized since the Second World War, the Japanese take great care not to make overstatements. To speak with reserve is thought paradoxically to be the best means of expressing the most. This peculiar characteristic of the Japanese, which is thought to be a rather graceful attainment, has often been labelled incorrectly as ambiguity and incomprehensibility. Moreover, when such understatement is sublimated and artistically refined, it enhances the art form of *Nōh*. Dr Scott Morton's advice then becomes both timely and worth paying attention to once the connection between *Nōh* and the Japanese temperament is accepted as given.

The art of *Nōh* shows 'movement in stillness' and in this drama 'the voice speaks in silence.' *Yūgen* is to be found here in such paradoxes. The actor in a *Nōh* play prefers to force us to grasp the whole action including the suggestiveness which lies behind and within those minor gestures resulting from the most restrained of physical movement. A plethora of words and gestures do not always touch a string of the heart. Rather 'the voice in silence' and 'a movement in stillness' can make a greater impression on the mind. The recognition of such a truth produces the magnetic quality of *yūgen*, so central to *Nōh*. We find the same understanding in Dōgen's statement in the chapter, *Ango* (*Training Period*) of the *Shōbōgenzō*: '*Gongo-dōdan* (beyond words) covers all words'; or in the chapter, *Kannon*: '*Hakku-jō* (80 or 90 per cent) is 100 per cent.' '*Gongo-dōdan*' was the Buddhist term usually used to mean the impossibility of understanding the truth of Buddhism, since it was so profound as to be 'beyond words'.

Dōgen, who grasped the negative truth of this phrase, dares to turn it paradoxically into a terse affirmation: 'Beyond words covers all words.' The meaning of '*hakku-jō*' as used in *Zen* is 'not enough or incapable of being fully grasped by words'. Dōgen again dares, as in the former case, to proclaim that even '80 or 90 per cent is 100 per cent' or 'complete'. 'Leaving something unsaid' results in 'expressing all' while 'leaving nothing unsaid' results in 'saying too much' or in 'overstatement'. The *Shōbōgenzō* depends upon a written style which 'left something unsaid'. The author takes care to use suggestive and economical expressions, while omitting detailed explanations or unnecessary basic premises. One of the best examples is found in the following statement in the chapter, *Bodaisatta-Shishō-Bō* (*Four Provisions according to which Bosatsu Urges Sentient Beings to Proceed Toward the Buddha Way*): 'Alms means "not to covet"; "not to covet" means "not to flatter".' The logical explanation is not fully given here about the connection between 'alms' and 'not to covet' and 'not to flatter'. An illogical, intuitive 'leap' on the part of the reader is demanded before the cryptic phrases blend into a full bodied truth.

In the *yōkyoku* of the *Nōh*, such intuitive acrobatics are often demanded, for example: 'night storm with snow' (*Tamura – The Shōgun Tamura*): 'it is snowing and raining' (*Kurama Tengu – The Long-Nosed Goblin of Mount Kurama*). At first glance, the reader is likely to interpret the section as a simple description of weather. But in reality it is a clever analogy suggesting cherry blossoms falling in the wind. *Nōh* playwrights deliberately use such a figure of speech in order to produce a more vivid impression of the scene. This mode of expression with its clever omission of details is a common feature of *yōkyoku* and the *Shōbōgenzō*. As the examples indicate it is not only physical matter which the playwright or priest/philosopher focuses on, but those more elusive realities beyond the limits of time and space. This quality of evanescence, of elusiveness is central to any understanding of *yūgen*.

Another example of the Japanese national characteristic, *yūgen*, is embodied in the noblest form of the Japanese sword, *Nihon-tō*. While *yūgen* is an aesthetic term peculiar to literary arts such as *Nōh*, it is not inappropriate to apply this same term to the sword. The beautiful form and colour of a master sword fascinates the mind, attracting it so strongly that a viewer is likely to be carried into the depths of the elegance and beauty it represents. And so, although the medium is different, the aesthetic experience of the beholder as he comes in contact with such refined beauty is the same as in *Nōh*. What should also be noted at this point is that the nature of something like Dōgen's *gūjin* can be discovered as well in the *Nihon-tō*, precisely because of the fact that the integration of the intellect and experience via intuition is realized in the artistic form of the sword. Contradictions stemming from cause and effect, matter and form give way to the intuitive power to penetrate to the core of the beauty which the inner eye perceives.

This integration is of the very essence of Dōgen's *gūjin* as well as the *Nihon-tō*. Symbolically, one may argue that the Japanese sword is the best concrete example of Dōgen's metaphysical approach to beauty. The integration of contradictions in the sword can be perceived in the harmony between form and function. Certainly a sword must be sharp as its function is to cut. But, for Japanese eyes, not only function but also form are essential factors in sword making. This, however, gives rise to a sort of contradiction, for in general a sword is made as a weapon and a weapon is likely to be awkward and almost brutal because of its primary function which is to kill. It is true that in other countries swords are traditionally manufactured because of this function, and it alone, while the *Nihon-tō* is made not only to function but to produce in the viewer a feeling of artistic beauty. Such a contradictory experience of harmony produced by disparate elements is characteristically Japanese. In Japan, a sword can never be considered to be excellently crafted until its dual functions as a work of art and a weapon are perfectly fulfilled. The finest blades have always been admired as cultural treasures, and examples of fine art. The *Nihon-tō* is a weapon, to be sure, but it embodies the aesthetic and the noble thus moving it beyond its function as a mere weapon. It represents the soul of the *samurai* (warrior), and the spirit by which life and death were confronted and set aside as problems, neutralized, and transcended through adherence to the Buddhist concept of *kū*. Careful reflection on the significance of the Japanese sword enables us to catch a glimpse of that spirit which animated Japanese society in the Middle Ages.

The fact that the Japanese sword is an example of the integration of knowledge and practice through intuition can be proven by the Japanese adage that the sword is 'trained' instead of 'forged' or 'tempered'. 'To train', *kitaeru* in Japanese, suggests stages of improvement, and a commitment to successive degrees of rigour which in turn leads to a specific goal. In forging the Japanese sword, hot steel is repeatedly struck, flattened out and folded sixteen times over. So if we cut across the blade and polish its cross-section, we may see a delicately beautiful pattern like the ever widening series of annual rings on the cross-section of a tree. The sword gradually brings itself to perfection by allowing itself to be tempered by the repeated blows from the hammer of the swordsmith. In this sense, a *Nihon-tō* is not merely the product of the refined technique of the swordsmith, it is the result of the integration of knowledge and practice through intuition; through intuition, because the method by which it is produced is not scientific but intuitional.

For an aspiring student swordmaker, an acquaintance with, even proficiency in, the chemical process is not enough. The essential non-material component which he must possess is intuition, carefully refined. This aesthetic intuition can only be grasped experientially by the pupil through disciplining by the Master. Because of this, the multiple techniques resulting in the creation of the Japanese sword have been passed on through the apprentice system which cultivates a strong spiritual bond between Master and pupil. It is often remarked that the traditional excellence of the *Nihon-tō* could never be reproduced by the sophisticated technology of contemporary methods. This is mainly because the swordsmith today lacks the same quality of experience as that of his counterpart in the past.

The problem is not one of technique but of the absence in the aspiring swordsmith of a refined sensibility which can only develop because of the rigorous disciplining of the Master. An appeal to intuition to bridge the gap between knowledge and action is essentially the same for aesthetic pursuits as well as for those of a religious nature. If one may now argue after such a lengthy discussion that the *kōan* in *Zen* can be essentially perceived as *yūgen*, then the *Shōbōgenzō*, Dōgen's monumental work is *yūgen*, because it is itself the theoretical explanation of *kōan* used by the student or novice in the art of *zazen*.

2 Climatic conditions

The previous section dealt with the uniqueness of Dōgen's thought which perceives profundity as *yūgen*. This understanding is based in turn upon a consideration of the racial characteristics of the Japanese themselves, as exemplified by two traditional arts, the manufacture of the Japanese sword and the *Nōh* play. Of course the Japanese sword and *Nōh* are not the only products of *yūgen*. They are merely two outstanding examples whose excellence compares well with Dōgen's thought. Many other cultural pursuits share in the common ground of beauty characterized or imperfectly described by their exquisite elegance, calm profundity, and fleeting quality. There is no need to deal with all the manifestations of *yūgen* in the culture. It is sufficient to inquire further into a basic element they all share. Such an investigation, in turn, will shed more light on the distinctive qualities of Dōgen's metaphysics. The point in question is that of climate.

As a backdrop for discussion, it is necessary to review the history of Japanese *Zen*. *Zen* made its appearance in Japan at the beginning of the thirteenth century, shortly before the birth of Dōgen, when a monk by the name of Eisai (or Yōsai, 1141-1215) transmitted the *Zen* practices of the *Rinzai* sect of China. From the thirteenth to the fourteenth century, many Chinese *Zen* masters of the *Rinzai* sect came to Japan as refugees, owing to the political disturbances in China which resulted in the overthrow of the Sung Dynasty. *Zen* thought exerted a far-reaching influence upon every aspect of Japanese culture: literature, the fine arts, architecture and *bushi-dō*, the code of the *samurai* warrior. It also underwent changes in Japan which resulted in an eclectic development which gave birth to many excellent cultural forms proper to Japan. Of these, *Nōh* and *yōkyoku* as a composite art form, the tea-ceremony and its distinctive style of architecture, Japanese landscape gardening, and *haiku* poetry remain alive even today in the everyday lives of the average Japanese. Dr Suzuki Daisetsu's contribution to introducing Japanese *Zen* to the West has resulted in many non-Japanese having a wide appreciation of the *Zen* underpinnings of traditional Japanese culture. One of them is *yūgen*.

In many cases, *yūgen* can be translated as 'mystery' in English, but 'mystery' refers to something supra-sensory, incomprehensible, beyond human understanding. In short, 'mystery' is often related to the idea of wonder. *Yūgen*, however, though it may or may not be rooted in agnosticism, makes one aware of the presence of something greater than is seen in what is manifest. *Yūgen* is not always accompanied by wonder. It makes the beholder feel the presence of something in nothingness, an experience which is rooted in an apparent contradiction. *Yūgen* may be closer to 'profundity' in English and yet it suggests a more supra-sensible reality than 'profundity'. As an attempt at some conclusion, it may be said that *yūgen* is a concept that rests astride both mystery and profundity.

Yūgen informs the art of *Nōh* as has been mentioned before. In fact, it may be conceded that the beauty of *yūgen* is peculiar to *Nōh* art. Some fundamental characteristics of this beauty, however, can be seen in various aspects of other cultural manifestations such as a rock garden, or the stark black and white *sumie* painting. The *wabi* or the *sabi* of the tea-ceremony and of a *haiku* poetry may also be linked to *yūgen*. A rock garden is deceptively simple: several rocks, small or large, are laid upon raked white sand. There are not plants, other than clusters of moss. But this simplicity, this deliberate understatement evokes in the mind of the beholder the grandeur of nature — the thunderous torrents of the waters, the swelling of the waves of the sea, woods, wild fields and high mountains. *Sumie* also evokes similar associations of richly coloured landscapes, of hills and waters all paradoxically etched on the mind in a vague, simple and monochromatic style of painting. In short these two arts lead to an enlarged capacity of mind which enables us to taste 'much in nothingness' or 'strong movement in stillness'.

Wabi and *sabi* are other examples of a similar type of 'affirmation in negativeness'. *Wabi* designates something devoid of practical value — something seemingly worthless that is the epitome of 'shabbiness' or 'poverty', i.e. *wabishisa* in Japanese. Paradoxically, because of this 'shabbiness', it leads to that which is of profound value, to a refined 'taste' for quietude and stillness. This is also the case with *sabi*. *Sabi* is derived from *sabishisa* and suggests the apparently negative meaning of 'lonesomeness', and yet it too converts into something noble, into a resigned almost contented sorrow in the face of beauty. These two terms are best applied to the tea-ceremony and *haiku* poetry. The tea-ceremony is the way through which one can acquire quietude and inner peace. In the modest and detached atmosphere of the tea-ceremony held in some rustic setting, even the slight sound of water simmering in a kettle conjures up the swaying motion of pines on some far away hill, and invites the participants to calm profundity, the *yūgen* of the immense cosmos.

The calm and solitude evoked by *wabi* and *sabi* can paradoxically become that which brings forth an intense, freeing energy which leads to great activity, just as the practice of *zazen* can produce an active spirit paradoxically because of its being grounded in stillness. There is an adage: 'The taste of *Zen* and the taste of tea are the same', which attempts to express how deeply involved the tea-ceremony is with *Zen*. In *haiku* poetry, we also find elements of *yūgen*. In *haiku* poetry, the apparently rigid tenets governing image and form result in an intense telescoping of the phenomena of nature which in turn exercises a profound impact on the mind of the poet and the reader. Although not as dynamic or obvious as *Nōh* or tea-ceremony, the poverty of language and imagery may be said to reveal something of the richness of *yūgen*. Motivated and enhanced by *Zen*, the original, aesthetic sense of the Japanese created these and other sophisticated art forms.

In a similar manner *yūgen* made its appearance in Japanese culture under the stimulus of *Zen*. But we may also argue that the quality of *yūgen* is itself inherent in the Japanese character. While *Zen* had its origin in India and developed more fully in China, it is logical to presuppose that the attraction for evanescence so central to *yūgen* ought to have appeared in both countries. The fact that only Japan gave rise to such a unique cultural value suggests that the Japanese possessed an inherent inclination toward it, and we may further say that this inclination was fostered by climatic conditions prevalent in Japan. As other scholars have argued, geography and the monsoon undeniably influenced the Japanese national character. Unlike continental China and India, which are also in a monsoon region, Japan, an island nation, has a comparatively high degree of humidity and four distinct seasons. The climate is changeable and the varied conditions result in a wide range of plant and tree life. Such natural phenomena can be considered to be and to foster a form of vagueness.

If we recognize the import of the constant interaction between the Japanese and nature, it then follows that such 'vagueness' is a major force in subtly forming their delicate sensibilities and national character. The Japanese have never been afflicted with the monotony of an unchanging topography. They have no experience of the cruel excesses of the weather, of bleak deserts, or barren fields and mountains. Theirs is a panorama of hills giving way to farmlands dipping into the sea, and of no clear barriers between land and ocean areas – all of which in turn supports an aesthetic and intuitive attachment to vagueness. Dōgen's thought can be reviewed in its affinity both to profundity commingled with evanescence and to that vagueness which is symptomatic of the climate of Japan. The difficulty of the *Shōbōgenzō* also derives from this same kind of vagueness.

One of the remarkable offshoots of *yūgen* fostered by natural phenomena is the awareness that nature and human nature are to be both one and in harmony. Several of the *yōkyoku* sing that, 'all the grasses, trees, and countries can become Buddha.' Dōgen also often made reference to the *Zen* phrase: 'the whole world is contained in the real body of man (*shinjitsu-nintai*).' These examples emphasize the point that the barriers between different modes of existence are not only blurred, they rather give way to union, to an almost quasi-mystical oneness. The excerpt from the *yōkyoku* is said to have been written in Japan, while the *Zen* inspired phrase was brought from China. But, the interpretation which the Japanese sought to find in this phrase was very peculiar to them, and cannot be grasped without some consideration of the natural context out of which the Japanese sensibility operates.

Dōgen was especially rich in the gift of perceiving the richness of natural beauty. This is proven by the fact that he composed several pieces of poetry on natural themes not because he stressed the significance of poetry – in fact, he denied it – but because he sought to express his own moments of *yūgen*. The following poem by Dōgen in the *Chokusen-waka-shū* (*Imperial Anthologies*) illustrates this point:

> On the ridge of the hills
> Dimly shines the moonlight.
> Fireflies are flitting
> In their pale light.

Such an immediate aesthetic grasp of natural beauty coexists alongside a tender regard for the fragility of such beauty. Dōgen discusses the concept of 'alms' in the chapter, *Shishōbō* and states that 'Flowers fall off their stalk when their time comes and birds sing according to the season.' He also argues that 'alms' may also mean, 'not to meddle in and break this working of nature.' Alms or *fuse* is a Buddhist term which means originally a physical offering to the poor as a token of the practice of *Bosatsu*. But, the fact that Dōgen applied this word even to flowers and birds enables us to see not only his extensive vision but also his rich sensibility nurtured by the climate of Japan. In order to grasp the profundity of Dōgen's teaching, it is necessary to be aware of the influence of the climate on Dōgen and his countrymen, while making an effort, at the same time, to appreciate the mystic sensibility fostered by the climate of Japan.

3 Contradiction and comprehensiveness

As has previously been noted, Dōgen often makes contradictory statements. For example, he teaches us that the gist of his precepts is nothing but sitting, *zazen*, whereas he puts special stress on *shiaku-shuzen* (the practice of doing good and refraining from doing evil) as if to say that the latter rather than the former is all that he intends to teach. In some places, he expounds the interpretation that women may attain Buddhahood, while in other places, he denies it. In the chapter, *Hotsu-mu-Jōshin* (*A Mind toward the Supreme Satori*) of the *Shōbōgenzō*, he praises the pious act of erecting a statue of the Buddha or the building of a pagoda as indicating the highest realization of the mind of *Bosatsu*. At the same time in the chapter, *Hotsu-Bodaishin* (*A Mind toward Practising the Way of Bodhisattva*) containing utterances recorded on the same dates as those above, he denies the significance of such acts of piety and attaches the highest value to the spiritual practice of *Bosatsu*. Other areas in which certain paradoxes emerge are those of poetry and literature. While he declares them insignificant, he displays a cultivated familiarity with both arts. References to similar contradictions have been made in earlier chapters of this book, but they will now be reconsidered as a distinctive facet of Dōgen's approach as a teacher.

The contradictory statements or behaviour itemized above may be explained away, as are the other examples, with either of the following explanations: (1) that the spiritual world cannot be grasped by simple, universal monistic principles; the mode of expression is relative, and depends upon the situation or the view-point which one takes, or (2) that there is always a certain distance between the ideal and the actual which necessarily leads to self-contradiction in speech and action. In the chapter on the *Genjō-kōan*, Dōgen states: 'If you bring only one side to the light, the other is dark.' 'The other is dark' intimates that total reality does not appear on the surface; it exists on another level although hidden from view. In another chapter of the *Shōbōgenzō*, *Uji* (*Existence and Time*) Dōgen advises us to allow for one more point of view: 'We cannot attain to total understanding from only a single reason.' As Dōgen stresses, as long as a multifaceted approach is taken to the matter under consideration, self-contradiction is possible; or at least the speaker will appear to put forth contradictory points of view. This holds true for Dōgen himself. If his teachings or even general comments are approached from a monistic point of view, the student/scholar will always fail to grasp the entire truth he expounds. A fuller, more involved approach is needed – one which accepts the premise that truth is never simplistic.

One case in point involves a series of quarrels among Dōgen's disciples arising from the problem of who was to be his true Dharma successor. The problem can be traced back to Dōgen's criticism of a priest by the name of Daie. Daie-Shūkō (1089–1163) was born about 100 years before Dōgen. As seen in section 3, chapter 2 of this book Daie was well known as a representative Master of *kōan-Zen* (*kanna-Zen*). Especially in his later years his fame was unrivalled throughout Japan. Even after his death, his religious teachings had great influence. While Dōgen was in China around the year 1220 Daie's influence was paramount. Dōgen, however, adopted a critical attitude towards Daie's approach. In the chapters, *Sesshin-Sesshō* (*The Explanation of the Mind and the True Nature of Man*) and *Jishō-Zanmai* (*To Acquire Satori by Self-reflection*), Dōgen expresses his unequivocal disapproval of Daie's formulation. Especially in the latter chapter, he went so far as to attack and severely rebuke Daie for not having sufficiently grasped the truth of *Zen* Buddhism. Such criticism of Daie is, however, necessarily ambiguous, because Dōgen allowed many disciples of the Daie school to study under him. One such pupil is Ejō, who had Dōgen's confidence and was subsequently appointed the second Chief Priest of the *Eihei-ji* temple. The same holds true of such successors as Gikai, the third, and Gien, the fourth.

There were many other competent disciples of the same school. Ejō had studied under Kakuan, who had received the mantle of Daie as his successor. Gikai and others had studied under Ekan, who had been the pupil of Kakuan. Certain elements of chance brought all of them to Dōgen. Taking these factors into consideration, it can be presumed that Dōgen all the more severely attacked Daie's *Zen* teaching, because he intended to impress his ex-Daie disciples with their errors and his own *mokushō-Zen* orthodoxy. Accepting this as a given then may clear up the matter of contradictory statements by Dōgen. But this does not necessarily hold good for the case of Gikai.

Gikai studied Daie's *Zen* thought under Ekan and even after becoming the disciple of Dōgen, he maintained his relationship with his former Master. In the course of this dual process, he was even clearly certified as the successor of Ekan making him the virtual Dharma-heir of *kōan-Zen*, which was antagonistic to *mokushō-Zen*. Dōgen must have been aware of this fact. Gikai recorded in detail in his *Shitchū-kikigaki*, also known as *Goyuigon-kiroku* (*The Record of What Gikai heard from Dōgen and Ejō*) Dōgen's concern and interrogation of him regarding his being chosen the successor of Ekan. According to this document, Gikai won the full confidence of Dōgen and later the administration of *Eihei-ji* was entrusted to him. Indeed, Gikai proved himself to be an exceptionally talented administrator. After the death of Dōgen, he was sent to China by Ejō in order to undertake a detailed study of the temple system there. Upon his return to Japan, he dedicated himself to the construction of the main buildings of *Eihei-ji* and their interiors. All of this was undeniably in conformity with Dōgen's dying wishes.

Taking all these facts into consideration, it is possible to say that Dōgen showed no favouritism towards those disciples whom he personally trained. He treated the disciples of other masters who later came to him with warmth and without prejudice. Moreover, he showed himself to be broad-minded enough to appoint these latter disciples to positions of trust. To be sure Dōgen levelled stern criticism against Daie's teaching of *Zen* but he did not deny the truths he found in it. He certainly knew that there was something to be learned from Daie if only certain errors were remedied. Originally Dōgen was a trainee of the same *Rinzai Zen* sect as Daie, but he was converted to *mokushō-Zen* through the teaching of Nyojō.

Another facet of Dōgen's personality and teaching to be noted is that he was a firm pacifist. According to *Shuryō-shingi* (*Rules for a Rest and Study House for Monks*) which Dōgen laid down, he banned monks from having arms in their temples under any pretext. Any offender against this rule was to be banished immediately from the temple precincts. It seems obvious that Buddhists should not take up arms, but, the fact of the matter was that some influential temples maintained soldier monks in case of attack. Taking such a historical fact into consideration, we have to regard Dōgen's prohibition against the taking up of arms as very significant. Again, the *Jū-undō-shiki* (The Rule in the Second Hall of *Zazen*) contains the disciplinary precept that: 'In a quarrel, both monks shall be expelled from the temple; those who witnessed the altercation and yet did not try to intervene will also be punished.' The severity contained in this rule was directed at both Dōgen himself, and the monastic order he governed.

An episode from Dōgen's life which underscores this fact is that the real reason for his removal at the age of 44 to *Eihei-ji* in Echizen, an area remote from Kyōto, was that he wanted to keep out of useless quarrels with other aggressive religious sects. Dōgen records the beginnings of such pacifism in *Shōbōgenzō-zuimonki*. While he was in Sung China, he had made up his mind not to quarrel with any man, under any pretext. He kept this secret vow all through his life. His criticism of Daie cannot be understood unless Dōgen's strong peace-loving attitude is seen to be at its centre. His severe attitude toward error was not based upon hate but rather concern for those who were in error. Dōgen was an amicable, broad-minded person whose tolerance found its source in the tolerance of Buddha. He further understood that the subtle discrimination of right from wrong was crucial when confronting error.

The concrete expression of such difficulty was the so-called *sandai-sōron* (the quarrel over the problem of who should be the third successor to the Chief Priest of *Eihei-ji*). Ejō, the second, legally abdicated 'the mantle' in favour of Gikai. But there was a faction who did not approve of his choice. They supported Gien who belonged, like Gikai, to the Daie school. Both had also been disciples of Dōgen. The conflict between the two groups was very intense. As a result Gikai was driven from *Eihei-ji* into retirement in another temple.

Much remains to be explained about this conflict, but two things can be put forth as causes. The first is the antagonism between the realists and the idealists among the monks concerning the way that the temple should be run. Gikai attached a great importance to actual missionary work in the name of the Dharma, while Gien stressed the primacy of one's devotion to 'sitting', *shikan-taza*, *i.e.*, an unworldly, idealistic exercise. The latter thrust explains the basis for the deep suspicion of Gien's group that Gikai was unfaithful to the school of *mokushō-Zen*. As was noted before, Gikai was the chief priest of *Eihei-ji* and yet he had received a certificate making him the legal Dharma-heir of *kōan-Zen*. This fact further intensified the suspicion among Gien's group that Gikai might not be faithful to *mokushō-Zen*. The suspicion necessarily led to hostility. These two underlying factors were the most probable causes of the problem.

They are, however, also to be traced back to the contradiction in Dōgen himself. The ambivalence found in the positions of the two factions manifested itself in Dōgen's teaching. As to the first cause, Dōgen strongly advocated *shikan-taza* but at the same time he stressed the need for missionary work. So if a monk were faithful to the former teaching of Dōgen, he could not but sympathize with Gien. If the focus were on the latter, one's sympathy transferred itself to Gikai. To try to be faithful to both inevitably led to contradiction. As to the emphasis on legal succession, it is known that Dōgen regarded this as being of primary importance. If so, Dōgen's approval of Gikai as Dharma-heir to the *kōan-Zen* school, while Gikai himself represented the school of *mokushō-Zen*, throws light on Gien's attack on Gikai. The more fundamental cause of the conflict may be attributed to the apparent contradictions in Dōgen's teachings and the narrow-minded approach of Dōgen's followers to their interpretation. The point to be taken note of here is that the various conflicts among Dōgen's disciples were somehow not resolved but assumed into the comprehensiveness of the Master's teaching. Interesting enough there arose no serious problem among the monks concerning the activity or management of the temple until after Dōgen's death when he was no longer present to reconcile troublesome opposites.

Some attention needs to be given to the quality of comprehensiveness alluded to here. It is marked by tolerance, inclusiveness, and none of the sharp dichotomizing of the Western mind. It is peculiarly Japanese as demonstrated by an eclecticism which persistently welcomes what other cultures and political systems have to offer, while at the same time seeming to avoid any possible ill-effects. For this trait the Japanese have often been unfavourably criticized as being a nation of imitators, granted that comprehensiveness may be but one step removed from imitation. But must imitation always be worthless? Not really, because by imitating the advances of Western culture, Japan has been able to achieve the rank, both politically and economically, of one of the great powers of the world. This was rapidly accomplished after Japan opened its doors to the West in the mid-nineteenth century. Also, it may be strongly argued that an inflexible attitude towards progress, and an inability to compromise would have made this impossible.

On the debit side, however, this imitation and flexibility of the Japanese also resulted in the discarding of certain traditional elements of Japanese life, and this with few qualms. This is to be regarded as a matter of great regret. But, setting aside the magnitude of this problem, the all inclusive quality of the Japanese mind may be said to have been fostered by some climatic condition found in Japan. This climatic condition, *yūgen*, which disposes the Japanese to almost dissolve themselves into their surroundings, has bred in them a sense of oneness with nature and a capacity for being receptive to everything around them without offering resistance. This in turn leads to a peculiar tolerance and an all-embracing, somewhat indiscriminating acceptance of things; but it also leads to imitation and a self-effacement peculiar to the Japanese. Whether this 'comprehensive mind' leads to a debilitating indiscriminateness, to foolish imitation which is lacking in originality, or develops into an altruistic spirit of tolerance and great benevolence, depends upon the way each person responds in a given situation. Dōgen's comprehensiveness is of the latter type; it is altruistic, highly refined and grounded in the culture of Japan as well as dependent upon Dōgen's own unique actualization of himself.

Another similar and equally important example linked to the problem of comprehensiveness is the fact that when the *Shōbōgenzō* was written, the language chosen was Japanese. At that period in Japanese history, Chinese was generally used for authoritative, academic and ceremonial writing. This practice presents another good illustration of the strength and weakness of the Japanese people. They imported Buddhism from China and studied it not in translation, but, in its original Chinese texts. This is in remarkable contrast to the Chinese who studied Buddhism after first translating texts from Sanskrit into their own language. The Japanese tried to remain faithful to the original Chinese, so much so that it became the general rule for the founders of the different sects or the priests of high rank to write commentaries of their works, especially the important ones, in Chinese. Dōgen broke with this practice. He wrote in Japanese. Some of his works were written in Chinese; the more important ones were written in Japanese. This was, for the time, an unprecedented practice. Naturally individual attempts did not completely get rid of the Chinese influence. The Japanese texts retain a stiffness; sentences are brief, a characteristic of Chinese, and not sufficiently coherent. All the technical terms related to the *kōan* are in Chinese. But, since the general trend was for the *Zen* masters to write in Chinese, Dōgen's challenge to tradition was singularly epoch-making. For the first time a Japanese wrote and explored foreign learning through the medium of his own language.

Dōgen's original insights into Buddhism were grounded in the essential fact of his being racially and culturally Japanese. Moreover the fact that Dōgen's comprehensiveness never leaned toward imitation as some Japanese are prone to do, ought to be especially significant. This was due in essence to the fact that his comprehensiveness was firmly rooted in an amazing discretion. His original interpretation of *dōji* in the chapter, *Shishō-Bō* of the *Shōbōgenzō* bespeaks this fact. Buddhism regards comprehensiveness as the most important component of *Bosatsu*. This is stressed by the practice called *dōji*. *Dōji*, according to its literal sense, means 'to accommodate ourselves to the things of others.' This points, however, to a paradoxical 'way' to attain Buddha-hood. *Dōji* is one of the four essential practices demanded of us in the way of *Bosatsu*. A contradiction is implied here because if we accommodate ourselves completely to the things of others, we will be carried away by them. At the same time self-hood is lost and the aim of attaining one's true self vitiated. In this sense, *dōji* should not be taken as a mere self accommodation.

Dōgen, perceiving this dilemma, put a new interpretation on *dōji*. He states that *dōji* means 'to accommodate ourselves to something' but it means 'to accommodate ourselves to the things of others at the same time as we accommodate ourselves to self.' He insists that this dual accommodation expresses the truth of *dōji*. Conflict inevitably arises if we attempt to accommodate ourselves to the things of others. In so doing, we cannot but annihilate ourselves, and vice versa. Nevertheless in *Bosatsu-dō* this difficult practice is demanded. Dōgen suggests a solution to the dilemma in the theory of *kū*. In the *Shōbōgenzō*, he adopted many *kōan* from the Chinese Patriarchs; but at the same time, he endeavoured not to lose his subjective self as a Japanese. This is exactly what Dōgen aimed at by writing this work in Japanese. By way of summation, comprehensiveness should not result in the loss of individuality or originality. Dōgen's statement on *dōji* that we should accommodate ourselves to the things of others at the same time as we practise self-accommodation should be accepted as a universal and practical principle. True harmony is achieved by bringing the comprehensive mind to bear on the many, apparent conflicts of life.[1]

Supplement

1 The works and writings of Dōgen

It need scarcely be said that the student of any philosophy or literature had best read the works in their original form. He ought to start his study by learning the language in which they are written. This is also the case with the study of Dōgen. Without a knowledge of Japanese the *Zen* Master remains elusive. This supplement will hopefully be of some help to those students who want to attempt a detailed study of Dōgen. The major works and writings of Dōgen are:

1 *Fukan-zazengi*, 1 vol.: the work was written soon after Dōgen returned from China. It is in the form of a manifesto to the world explaining how he set up his new sect on the basis of the practice of *zazen*.

2 *Hōkyō-ki*, 1 vol.: this work records the dialogue between the author and his master, Nyojō, during the Hōkyō period in Sung China. It provides an introduction to the fundamental character of Dōgen's thought.

3 *Dōgen-oshō-kōroku*, generally known as *Eihei-kōroku*, 10 chapters: a collection of the various precepts of the author.

4 *Gakudō-yōjin-shū*, 1 vol.: this practical study centres around an approach to the study of Buddhism and the practice of *zazen*.

5 *Sanshō-dōei*, also known as *Dōgen-zenji-waka-shū*: Dōgen's poetical works are collected into an anthology of *waka*.

6 *Shōbōgenzō-zuimonki*, 6 chapters: this is a first hand record of the Master's precepts relating to his daily life and recorded by one of his followers.

7 *Shōbōgenzō*, 87 or 95 chapters: these are original studies and lectures by the author on various problems concerning Dharma and the basis of *kōan*.

Note: The works cited above will be of special help to any study which takes a philosophical approach to Dōgen's thought. Other works, dealing with the historical and specific contexts of Dōgen's thought or certain more specialized problems, may be needed for reference, but automatically in the process of your wider and deeper study of such problems, such books will surface; so I may be permitted to omit a direct reference to them here.

The authoritative published versions of the above books are:

Sōtō-shū-zensho, 33 vols, published by *Sōtō-shū-zensho* kankōkai, Tokyo, 1977.

Dōgen-zenji-zenshū, 2 vols, Chikuma-shobō, Tokyo, 1969, 1970.

These two collections are complete. Both cover all the texts mentioned above from (1) through (7) as well as other secondary source materials. By way of footnotes, they are more suitable for the trained scholar.

Iwanami Library editions are the best available for general students in this regard. They are handy, with proper notes, comments and translations of the Chinese characters. One of these editions, entitled *Dōgen-zenji-goroku* includes (1) (4) and (5) from the cited works, You can also find the *Hōkyō-ki* and the *Shōbōgenzō-zuimonki* in this library edition.

Dōgen-oshō-kōroku is included in the *Eihei-kōroku-chūkai-zensho*, 4 vols (including a one volume index) published by Kankōkai, Tokyo, 1975; it is to be recommended as being easily available. *Eihei-kōroku* appears in modern Japanese as: *Yakuchū-eihei-kōroku* with notes by Yokoi Yūhō under the design of Sankibō-busshorin, Tokyo, 1978.

The *Shōbōgenzō* numbers several versions, but the following ones can be safely recommended as standard works:

1 *Shōbōgenzō* by *Iwanami* Library edition, 3 vols. This is handy and includes an index and a dictionary.

2 *Shōbōgenzō* in the fifth volume of Religious Sect of *Shōwa-shinsan-kokuyaku-daizōkyō*, published by Tohō-shoin, Tokyo, 1929. This is very readable with simplified Japanese *kana* (readings) for all Chinese characters. The problem of a correct reading for the Chinese characters still exists but the decision made by the editors is reasonably authoritative.

3 *Kohon-kōtei-Shōbōgenzō*, edited by Ōkubo Dōshū, Chikuma-shobō, Tokyo, 1971 and generally known as the *Chikuma version*, is notable for the excellent explanatory notes for the text as well as for its order of chapters.

One further piece of advice is that one should acquire some background knowledge of the composition of the *Shōbōgenzō* before reading it. As we have already seen in Chapter 1 of this book, the number of chapters of the *Shōbōgenzō* is not definite; each version has its own order and holds to a different number of chapters *e.g.* 12, 28, 60, 75, 95 chapters etc. The composition pattern which Dōgen finally set down is supposed to be that of 75 chapters with an additional 12 chapters added on, though some scholars think he might have planned it to be a work totalling 100 chapters in all. It is only in the post-war era that this opinion has come to be generally accepted. Since the Edo era the theory that the total work consisted of 95 chapters had been thought to be correct. The so-called *Honzan version* is based upon this view. The *Shōbōgenzō* versions found in the *Iwanami* Library edition and in the fifth volume of Religious Sect of *Shōwa-shinsan-kokuyaku-daizōkyō* are also based upon the same view, but the former includes one additional chapter which was discovered in the Shōwa era. The *Chikuma version* is composed of 75 chapters plus an additional 12 chapters, and one addendum. This may be closer to the original intention of Dōgen himself. Indeed the content is better systematized in this version than in other ones. The 95-chapter version is compiled chronologically, an added benefit to the reader. At any rate, the composition pattern of chapters does not matter so much for the student who has some background knowledge as mentioned above.

2 Notebooks

Of all Dōgen's works the *Shōbōgenzō* is by far the most difficult one to understand. If you master Japanese, it is relatively simple to read other philosophical or religious works without too much trouble. You can rely upon good notes and use modern Japanese version. But the *Shōbōgenzō* is an exception. Often, even translations or notes may not help you at all. It is not an exaggeration to say that the content of all 95 chapters is beyond general understanding. This may be due to the following two points: firstly, when Dōgen preached on the words and actions of the Patriarchs as *kōan*, he did not treat them in their literal and superficial meaning but, always tried to reach out to their innermost truth; secondly, the background and the premises on which his precepts on *kōan* are based are not explained, or if explained at all, only tersely as a fact or truth which is taken for granted. Therefore in order to grasp exactly what the author means in this monumental work, the reader must often trace the quotations back to their original source and reconsider them from the point of view of Dōgen's speculations.

Some earlier commentators have made minute and laborious studies and left us with the fruit of their labour. Such material is grouped under the general heading of *Old Notes* and distinguished from recent annotators, *New Notes*. A line of demarcation between the two is drawn in the latter part of the Edo era. But the *Shōbōgenzō-keiteki*, 2 vols, published in the Mieji era, is a fine academic notebook, esteemed as highly as the *Old Notes*. Today these notebooks are available in the more readable form of 3 volumes.

There are some seven kinds of authoritative books included under the *Old Notes*, covering commentaries by Dōgen's immediate pupils who attended his lectures. *Shōbōgenzō-chūkai-zensho*, 11 vols, published by Kankōkai, Tokyo, 1975 contains not only the commentaries but also annotations, comments, and reference sources. Sometimes one may have to consult old manuscripts to find out on which sources these *Old Notes* and commentaries are based, but the *Shōbōgenzō-chūkai-zensho* will satisfy nearly all your needs. The *New Notes* are often described in reference to the *Old Notes* and so sometimes you may have to be accurate in indicating to which *Old Notes* the *New Notes* refer. In case you cannot agree to any of the interpretations offered by the *Old Notes*, put forward your own comments, providing there are adequate textual reasons. This is the way taken by any scholar.

3 Authority of the kōan

The *Shōbōgenzō* puts forward Dōgen's own theory about the various problems concerning the Dharma on the basis of *kōan*. Therefore in order to understand this work, you often have to delve into the authority behind the *kōan*. When *kōan* are old traditional ones (*kosoku-kōan*), they are mostly those of Buddha's precepts, or if not, based upon the words and actions of the older Patriarchs. Most of the former are derived from Buddhist Scriptures and the latter from *Zen* books. The standard version of the Buddhist Scriptures for reference is: *Taishō-shinshū-dai-zōkyō*, often known only as *Taishō-zōkyō*, 100 vols, published by Kankōkai, Tokyo, 1977. You can read these scriptures in Japanese in one of the following three versions:

Kokuyaku-issaikyō, 255 vols, Daitō-shuppan, Tokyo.

Kokuyaku-daizōkyō, 31 vols, Daiichi-shobō, Tokyo, 1974.

Shōwa-shinsan-kokuyaku-daizōkyō, 48 vols, Tōho-shorin, Tokyo, 1931.

Zen books are composed mainly of remarks and biographical anecdotes of the old Patriarchs, so that they are frequently referred to as a source of information on the authority of the *kosoku-kōan*. *Dainippon-zoku-zōkyō* or more simply *Manji-zoku-zōkyō*, 150 packs, Zōkyō, Kyoto, 1912, contains most of these comments and anecdotes attributed to the *Zen* Patriarchs. A newer version, *Shinsan-dainippon-zokuzōkyō*, 100 vols, is now being published by the Kokusho-kankōkai. They are so essential for the study of the *Shōbōgenzō* that without them, the serious scholar will not be able to advance. *Dainippon-bukkyō-zensho* published by Kōdansha, Tokyo, 1972, is no less essential than the above collection. As to books about *Zen*, the following Japanese publications will prove helpful: *Kokuyaku-zenshū-sōsho*, 22 vols, Daiichi-shobō, Tokyo, 1974 and *Kokuyaku-zengaku-taisei*, 25 vols, Nishōdō shoten, Tokyo, 1930.

There are many other reference books of note, but it is not necessary to mention them here. They will naturally come to light as one's study advances.

Notes

1 Dōgen's life and his essential precepts

1 The age of a person in this study is given according to the Japanese way of reckoning birthdays, i.e. from New Year to New Year.

2 In Kant's philosophy we find the idea of 'a law for a law.' For him any element of a moral system, for instance, goodness is to be derived from the duty of pure will, that is to say, 'a duty for a duty'. Originally duty means legal obligation. Therefore 'a duty for a duty' leads theoretically to 'a law for a law'. Kant insists that morality should be based upon a pure objective criterion, not upon concrete reality such as personal happiness in one's daily life. The moral will of the individual ought to be pure. We find the same philosophical bias in Dōgen's idea of 'zazen for zazen'. The difference is, however, that Dōgen tries to locate this purity of the moral will in the practice of zazen. He does not posit a theoretical explanation of it. By juxtaposing the two philosophers it becomes clear that Kant's approach is analytical, theoretical and methodical, while Dōgen's is synthetical, intuitional, and therefore, in a sense, irrational.

3 As for the term, kufū (to seek the Buddha's true teaching), Dōgen scholars are likely to limit it to a special concept related to zazen. But this does not seem to fit in with the whole structure of Dōgen's thought. Kufū should be grasped in a more generic sense as concerning human will.

2 Genjō-kōan (the actuality of instruction)

1 The English equivalent for genjō-kōan is generally given as 'actualization is truth' or 'the actualization of enlightenment' but, through a close investigation of Dōgen's thought, the author finds this inappropriate. Genjō should be rendered 'actuality', and kōan 'instruction'.

The reader will grasp the significance of such a distinction from the discussion in this work.

3 Practice

1 *Kū* seems to be an important principle of the purity of intention at which practitioners of *Zen* try to arrive. This problem ought to be considered in greater detail by referring to Kant's understanding of *purity* mentioned in note 2, Chapter 1. Kant suggests the following view of the virtue of charity in one of his books, *The Metaphysical Principles of Virtue, Part II, of the Metaphysics of Morals*: 'To be charitable to the other person – to promote his happiness according to one's capacity without hoping for something in return is everyone's duty.' What we should take notice of in this statement is the contradiction in his ethical position of deontology. Here Kant betrays evidence of utilitarian teleology in spite of his strong denial of it, because he expects after all some practical result even from a person's purely ethical action as the phrase, 'to promote his happiness' reveals.

Originally 'a duty for a duty' may not bear true in theory. As we saw already, 'a duty for a duty' links itself to 'a law for a law'. If this logic is carried to an extreme, it meets such conflicts as 'measure for measure'. Measure is not for measure. It is an instrument used for measuring. The pure abstract quality of Kant's ethical theory gives way to such irrationality.

In the above statement, Kant stresses the phrase 'without hoping for something in return.' This may be what Kant has to say; any moral action should be unconnected with any desire for self aggrandizement. Dōgen's *kū* is exactly the same as Kant in this respect. Dōgen's instruction in *Zuimon-ki* quoted in *Iwanami* Library Editions will prove this: 'The primary requisite for the followers of Buddha is to leave self-centeredness' (p. 55). But the theory of duty as an act of pure will may sometimes go against natural inclination. A charitable act from pure duty may possibly disregard the heart of the object of such charity and even turn out to be harmful to one after all. Kant's formative ethics is likely to lay so much stress on purity, that it may disregard the real facts. In practice what is expected in our daily lives is not an abstract type of morality but, real results from it. This is the reason why Kant cannot but adhere to a utilitarian teleology after all, though this involves him in contradiction.

In contrast to Kant's pure ethics, *kū* takes the real very much into consideration, and yet it dares to transcend it. The practitioner of *kū* wishes happiness to some wretched person out of real sympathy and will share joy with him when it is attained. This is true charity.

Kū sets much value on the real way of morality, but at the same time it tries to transcend it so that worldly matters such as fame or profit are quite foreign to it. It aims at, in a sense, a purity which transcends purity itself. Dōgen's *goga-ridatsu* is a precept which hopes for the moral of the absolute purity based on *kū*.

4 On Buddha

1 There is some doubt as to whether the Genjō version of the Shingyo was truly Genjō's translation. Tradition says that Genjō translated the Sanskrit version into Chinese in AD 649. But there is evidence against this, in that the same translation had been handwritten by Ō-Yōjun in AD 635 while Genjō was in India. (Cf. Yamamoto Kūgai: *Spiritual Art and Religion*, published by Kōmyō-shūdō-kai in Kobe, March, 1981, p. 227.) But this problem seems too complex to discuss in detail here, so I only mention it for you to keep in mind for your future studies.

2 The exact title of this chapter is *Bodaisatta-Shishō-Bō*. This is not found in the version consisting of 75 volumes which was allegedly composed by Dōgen himself. But it may safely be said that the Chapter is undeniably Dōgen's own work. The content is worthy of this assumption. Therefore it ought to be treated as an important part of the *Shōbōgenzō*. *Bendōwa*, mentioned already in Chapter 1, p. 3, *Shōji*, and *Yuibutsu-Yobutsu* mentioned later in Chapter 4, pp. 41–3, are similar in source.

5 Gūjin (thoroughness) and Buddha

1 Regarding *shitsu-u-busshō*, there are some questions to be discussed. One of them is: if there is Buddha-nature in all sentient-beings, is it then unnecessary for us to go to the trouble of going through the practice of *zazen* to attain Buddhahood? This is the point most commonly misunderstood about *shitsu-u-busshō*. The answer to this question is offered in *Shinjin-Gakudō* (*To study the Buddha Way with Body and Soul*), Chapter 4 of the *Shōbōgenzō*. In this chapter, Dōgen tells us that if we don't study the Buddha Way with both body and soul, we can never realize Buddhahood even though it is inherent in us. This is exactly what the term, *sokushin-zebutsu* (our mind is itself Buddha) means. *Sokushin-Zebutsu*, Chapter 5 of the *Shōbōgenzō* elucidates the process. If the mind truly becomes Buddha through such study, it will unconsciously manifest itself in our daily lives. This is called *iigi*. *Gyōbutsu-Iigi* (*To Train Oneself in*

the Buddha Way and Take on the character of Buddha), Chapter 6, also elucidates this process. *Ikka-Myōju (One shining Ball)*, Chapter 7, goes a step further into the problem, and explains that each individual person has his own unique existence which is like a shining ball. In this way, the *Shōbōgenzō* develops its theory step by step into a grand design. In short, Dōgen claims that the world of Buddha can be realized only through practice.

6 Racial ground

1 From Chapter 4 on, several Oriental arts and their unique nature are treated on the basis of *Zen* thought such as *kū, yūsoku-ichinyo* (integration into one), synthesis of conflicts, intuitional practice. But calligraphy should not be forgotten as one of the most sophisticated arts of *Zen*. In regard to this art, the following study should be given special attention: *Shoron-taikei (Systematic Study of Calligraphy)*, pp. 108–47, one part of *Kūgai-bokuseki* published by Matsuyama Kōmyō-kai, Matsuyama, Ehime Prefecture, February, in 1980. Here the philosophy of a calligraphy is systematized from the universal point of view. This is an excellent study which will surely give you an important basis for understanding the thought of Dōgen.

Index of persons

Index of works

General index

Index